The Buildi

HERIOT-WATT
UNIVERSITY
EDINBURGH

Department of Building Engineering & Surveying

The Buildings Around Us

Thom Gorst

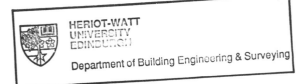

E & FN SPON
An Imprint of Chapman & Hall

London · Glasgow · Weinheim · New York · Tokyo · Melbourne · Madras

Published by E & FN Spon,
an imprint of Chapman & Hall,
2–6 Boundary Row,
London SE1 8HN, UK

Chapman & Hall,
2–6 Boundary Row,
London SE1 8HN, UK

Blackie Academic & Professional,
Wester Cleddens Road,
Bishopbriggs,
Glasgow G64 2NZ, UK

Chapman & Hall GmbH,
Pappelallee 3,
69469 Weinheim,
Germany

Chapman & Hall USA,
One Penn Plaza, 41st Floor,
New York NY 10119, USA

Chapman & Hall Japan,
ITP Japan,
Kyowa Building, 3F,
2-2-1 Hirakawacho,
Chiyoda-ku,
Tokyo 102, Japan

Chapman & Hall Australia,
Thomas Nelson Australia,
102 Dodds Street,
South Melbourne, Victoria 3205,
Australia

Chapman & Hall India,
R. Seshadri,
32 Second Main Road,
CIT East, Madras 600 035,
India

Cover shows Mercers House, London
Photograph: Martin Charles
Frontispiece: Tabard Gardens Estate, London

First edition 1995

© 1995 Thom Gorst

Typeset in Univers by Florencetype Ltd,
Stoodleigh, Devon
Printed in Great Britain at The University Press, Cambridge

ISBN 0 419 19330 8

A catalogue record for this book is available from the British Library

∞ Printed on acid-free text paper, manufactured in accordance with ANSI/NISO Z39.48-1992 (Permanence of Paper)

Contents

Introduction

In 1980 I moved into a flat in Camberwell, in the London borough of Southwark. Although I had completed my architectural training, and had a degree in Art History besides, I felt completely unqualified to understand the mix of buildings that formed the environment around my new home: there were warehouses and prefabs, and endless estates of council tenement blocks. No book I knew had tried to explain how these buildings came to be the way they were. So, for an hour every morning, before I went to my work in an architects' office, I systematically cycled down every road in the borough, photographing and making notes about each building I saw.

When I had finished this immensely rewarding project, I realized that I had learned much more about the history of architecture and building than I have ever learned in all my years of scholarship at college and university.

Above all, I had learned two most important principles: first, that architecture is about the buildings that surround us; and second, that the best way of understanding architecture is through observation and comparison.

When I used to visit local primary schools in the area, teachers often said that there was nothing of interest to see nearby, so there was no point in going to have a look. Who persuaded them that this was so? Who said that the only buildings worth looking at are stately homes and palaces? Such a view alienates people from their environment, and it belittles their own ability to say how they would like that environment to develop.

Through the selection and comparison of a wide range of buildings, this book repeats the discoveries of my Southwark tour by establishing the view that all building design constitutes architecture, and that all opinions about that architecture are equally valid.

Buildings 'speak' to us. They tell us about the economic and social structures of the times in which they were built. They speak of pride of ownership, of municipal or state power, and of commercial success – all through the subtle use of architectural form and decoration.

It has been, and still is, the job of the architect to understand the ways in which these messages can be communicated. It is not helpful to think of the architect as an artist whom we must struggle to understand and who alone holds the key to our comprehension of building design. The architect, like the advertising agent or the car designer, creates images with and on buildings that are intended to be understood by us all. The 'architect-designed' housing estate must clearly appeal to the people who are going to buy the houses. Equally legible are the images of a slick city-centre office block: here the messages may be more to do with asserting power, progress, security and confidence, and as such may not necessarily be the sorts of messages people will willingly want to hear. So architecture may impress, and it may also alienate. It is an urban cacophany, in which interests that have the power to create buildings are using those buildings to communicate very potent messages to the population generally, the majority of whom do not have the power to commission buildings.

Conventional thinking about architecture is highly judgemental: there are supposed to be good buildings, and bad ones. This view reinforces the position of the architect: it turns the architect into the only person who has enough training to discern the good from the bad. Without the benefit of that training, everyone else will have a flawed judgement. Not only do architects revel in this myth, but it is a myth that most of the rest of us willingly support. During my years as a housing architect and a teacher, I have been surprised at how unready people are to express their own views about the built environment. They often prefer to defer to the qualified architect, even though they have been actively engaging with the built environment for the whole of their lives.

This book introduces buildings without making these judgements, which so dangerously reinforce the myth of architecture as an élitist subject, and alienate the rest of society from the buildings that surround it. The book is concerned about one thing only – the built environment that we live in. It is not interested in still-born projects, or the secret intentions of architects; it is concerned with what is there, whether good or bad.

It is concerned with the 'popular environment': the environment that surrounds us all. But it does not fall into the trap of believing romantically in a 'popular culture' of architecture. The question of whether or not there is such a thing has received almost no academic attention, due, I suspect, to the immense control that the architectural profession exerts over cultural debate about the built environment.

While I am convinced that buildings are designed to interact on a cultural level with all of us, and the nature of that interaction must be understood by us all before we can take a significant part in environmental politics, I also believe that any notion of a popular culture within building disappeared with the rise of 'architecture' a century and a half ago.

Our preferences now are generated by the 'great' buildings that in some way articulate our aspirations – it is the same in our choice of cars, and our choice of dress. John Ruskin complained of the grotesque parodies of his own work that had sprung up in the south London suburbs, and John Betjeman talked about how modern homes were crude copies of the things we had seen in our masters' houses in the days when we were servants. As H. J. Dyos put it: 'Architectural taste, like manners, travels downwards.'

But, with each step it takes downwards, it is modified in a significant way. Therefore the 'Gothic' that we find on a suburban house is different from the Gothic that we find in a medieval cathedral, and the two cannot stand qualitative comparison with each other. The suburban house is not a crude copy, but an accurate reflection of the culture it was built for. When we criticize the suburban house, we are really criticizing the people who live in it.

A sample of 50 buildings is not nearly enough to represent all the different types, ages and locations of buildings within the contemporary environment, so this book can make no claim to be comprehensive. Whole areas are not represented, some building types are conspicuously (and even intentionally) absent, and many household-name architects are not mentioned at all. The selection of buildings introduces the issues that have shaped our built environment: through them we learn about legislation and technologies, and most of all we learn through comparison how building design has evolved over the last turbulent century and a half.

R. W. Brunskill, in his *Illustrated Handbook of Vernacular Architecture* (1978), pointed out that a building's chances of survival depend very much on its status within society. So it is that in our present environment we have examples of cathedrals that are nearly 1000 years old, but almost no examples of workers' housing that is 200 years old. The further we look back, the less representative the surviving buildings are of their own age. Comparisons of Ordnance Survey maps of urban areas show how quickly the constituents of the urban scene change.

Generally, buildings have about the same life expectancy as human beings. So, if our interest is in the environment that surrounds us today, we will find very few surviving buildings over 150 years old. In any case, the substantial changes in building technology that took place around 1850 – developments in heating and lighting, the mass production and distribution of building materials, and the introduction of comprehensive laws governing building construction – rendered the older environment largely obsolete.

By far the most common building type is the domestic house. It is therefore right that it should be the most frequently discussed type in this book. Then come offices, shops and municipal buildings: we engage with these at a day-to-day level, and their architecture inevitably engages with us. The problem is the church. It is a paradox that the church is deemed to be the most significant urban building type: Nikolaus Pevsner's impressive 'Buildings of England' series lists the churches in each town before all other building types. It does so because they are the 'special' buildings. But we are not interested here in special buildings; we are interested in understanding the 'language' that ordinary buildings use. If anybody feels that churches are under-represented in this book, then please refer to Pevsner, where the imbalance is more than redressed.

How to use this book

Mercers House, London.

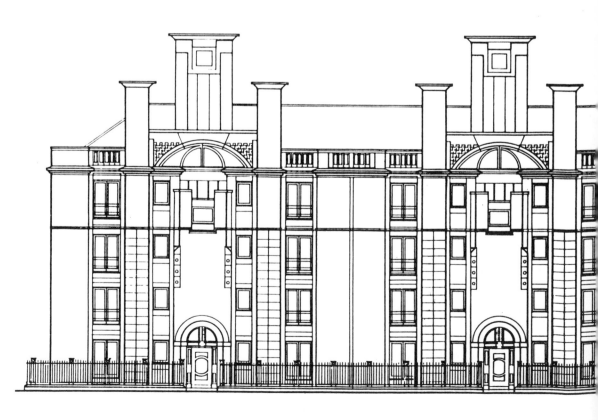

The main text in each of the 50 sections is a self-contained discussion about a building. When particular points raised by the building need further discussion, these are laid out next to the main text as topics. Points discussed as topics are printed in **bold**. Often, points that are mentioned either in the main text or in the topics have a particular relevance elsewhere in the book: these cross-references are placed in their own box, in alphabetical order.

You can use the book in a number of ways – you can work from beginning to end chronologically, or you can meander, flitting from one cross-reference to the next. Make the right choice, and the book will never end – you can become immersed in a spiral of architectural history, flying from the Vernacular to the Brutal as easily as you would from London to Cardiff.

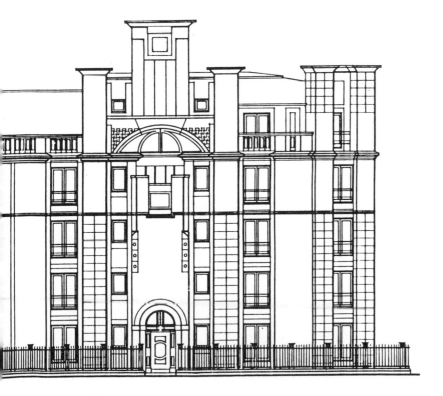

Acknowledgements

I would like to make brief but very sincere thanks to everyone who has encouraged me with this, my first book. I would especially like to extend my gratitude to the following: to Paul Woodhead of Bermondsey, with whom I set up an architecture workshop, and we discovered that the right book had not yet been written; to my old friends in the Coin Street Design Team, who helped me to find out what architecture really was all about; to Uncle Christopher of Southwark Architects, who made such positive comments on the early drafts; to everyone at my publishers, from the commissioning staff to the production and design teams, who gave me confidence in myself and faith in them; to the late Bastiaan Valkenburg of Kingston Polytechnic, a great teacher of architecture; to my parents; and to Teresa and Hannah, to whom the book is dedicated – to all of you, thank you.

Illustration acknowledgements

The author and publishers would like to thank the following individuals, organizations and publishers for permission to reproduce material. We have made every effort to contact copyright holders, but if any errors have been made we would be happy to correct them at a later printing.

Individuals and organizations

Alan Blanc; Building Design Partnership; Martin Charles; Coventry City Council; Russ Craig; Alan Day; Brian Edwards; Essex County Council; Hampshire County Council Architects Department; John Lewis Partnership; The National Trust for Scotland; Rangers Football Club; Selfridges Ltd; Tinh Lam; Brenda Vale; David Wrightson

Publications

The Architects Journal, EMAP, London

The Architectural Review, EMAP, London

Architecture Today, Architecture Today plc

Atwell, D. (1984) *Cathedrals of the Movies*, The Architectural Press, London

Beddington, N. (1990) *Shopping Centres*, Butterworth Heinemann, Oxford

Cruickshank, D. (1985) *A Guide to Georgian Buildings of Britain and Ireland*, Weidenfeld & Nicolson/The National Trust/The Irish Georgian Society

Dixon, R. and Muthesius, S. (1985) *Victorian Architecture*, Thames and Hudson, London

Edwards, A. (1981) *The Design of Suburbia*, Essex Design Guides, Pembridge Press Ltd

Howard, E. (1898) *Tomorrow: a peaceful path to social reform*, Thames and Hudson, London

GLC (1983) *The Urban School*, The Architectural Press, London

Gomme, A. and Walker, D. (1968) *The Architecture of Glasgow*, Lund Humphries, London

Nicholas Grimshaw & Partners (1988) *Book 1 Product*, Nicholas Grimshaw & Partners, London

Hughes, Q. (1964) *Seaport*, Lund Humphries, London

Jackson, A. (1970) *The Politics of Architecture*, The Architectural Press, London

Le Corbusier (1970) *Towards a New Architecture*, The Architectural Press, London

Letchworth Garden City (1911, republished 1986) *Guide to Garden City*

Whittick, A. (1974) *European Architecture in the 20th Century*, Leonard Hill Books, Aylesbury

Zevi, B. (1985) *Eric Mendelsohn*, The Architectural Press Ltd, London

Hamilton Square, Birkenhead 1830

The Renaissance

The word 'Renaissance' refers to the 'rebirth' of classical values and forms throughout the arts in the early 15th century, replacing those of the medieval period.

One of the first architects to reuse the forms of ancient Rome was Filippo Brunelleschi, whose design for the Ospedale degli Innocenti, Florence, of 1419 has been regarded as the first Renaissance building.

The terraced house emerged as a building type in Britain in the 18th century, combining in a completely new way the architecture of the Italian **Renaissance** with the repetitive form of rows of identical houses.

The houses that line the four sides of Hamilton Square are typical of the type. Birkenhead's prosperity grew from the 1820s, when its docks started to be developed, and William Laird established a shipbuilding yard on the Birkenhead side of the River Mersey.

The town was planned on a rectangular grid system, and the main public open space on the grid was Hamilton Square, which was to be surrounded by fine houses, with a new town hall in the centre of the west side.

The houses were built in phases from 1824–44, with minor variations between them. The architect was James Gillespie Graham, who had done much work in Edinburgh's New Town, and it has been said that the Hamilton Square houses have a distinctly Scottish look to them. The houses that surround Hamilton Square are only three windows wide, and it is almost impossible to ascertain where one ends and another begins. Only the front doors interrupt the regular pattern of windows on the façade. Consequently, each side of the square looks like one huge building – the individuality of each house has been suppressed, for the sake of the architectural integrity of the composition as a whole.

The evolution of the Georgian house façade from its classical origins: (a) the façade of Palladio's Palazzo Thiene, Vicenza, 1545, showing plinth, columns and entablature; (b) Palazzo Thiene reinterpreted at Covent Garden Piazza, London, 1630 (now demolished); (c) Hamilton Square, Birkenhead.

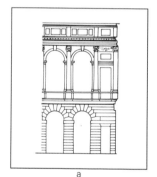

a

b

c

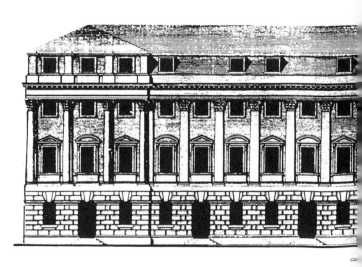

This method of composition was learned from the Italian Renaissance, and in particular from the work of the 16th-century architect Andrea **Palladio**, who had built many palaces and villas in Venice and the Vicenza area. He had reinterpreted the classical architecture of Greece and Rome for use in the domestic buildings of the new Venetian merchant classes, and he had demonstrated how all of the functions of a house could be gathered into one architectural composition.

This type of composition is termed **palazzo**, which is the Italian word for the great merchant palaces that were constructed in the heart of a town. To look now at, say, the Palazzo Thiene in Vicenza (built in 1545), it is hard to realize how important a building it was, for it has been studied and copied so many times.

When the Covent Garden Piazza in London was laid out in the 1630s, the design of the buildings around it bore a close resemblance to the Palazzo Thiene. Later palazzo compositions in Britain, such as the north side of Queen Square, Bath, of 1729, were given added dignity by emphasizing the centre and the two ends of the composition with further pediments.

But as the palazzo approach evolved, it was allowed to become plainer: frequently the central and end pediments would be left out, as would the large columns, which were copied from the Palazzo Thiene's façade. At Hamilton Square the composition is bare by comparison with the Palazzo Thiene. There are no giant

Palladio

Andrea Palladio (1508–80) was active in Venice and the surrounding area from about 1550. He had studied the architecture of classical Rome, and had used his knowledge to adapt that architecture to the needs of the modern buildings of the time.
His work falls into three groups: the design of urban palazzos, mostly in Vicenza; the design of rural and agricultural villas in the countryside around Vicenza; and the design of churches in the city state of Venice.
The Vicenza palazzos were

The Palazzo Thiene, Vicenza: Andrea Palladio, 1546.

designed to be the city homes and places of business for wealthy families, and their architectural treatment generally adhered to the archaeological precedents of ancient Rome.
Palladio's rural villas were often designed as complete farmyards, all gathered into one architectural composition based on classical Roman principles. But their novelty lay in the fact that the dwelling block frequently had a **portico** or 'temple front' attached to it.

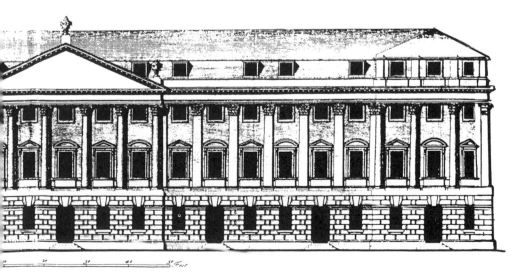

The façade of Queen Square, Bath, 1729, with a pediment in the centre and additional emphasis at the ends.

The most famous of these villas is the Rotonda of 1550, which was not really a farm, but more of a country retreat. It has four identical temple fronts attached to each of its four sides, and was imitated by Colen Campbell in 1722 at Mereworth Castle, and by Lord Burlington in 1725 at Chiswick House.

The Venetian churches are remembered primarily for their façades, which were extraordinarily successful in combining the idea of a Roman temple front, which is really a box with a roof on it, with a Christian church, with its high nave and two lower side aisles, by layering one low temple front on to another high one. This idea of layering and combining classical forms was developed by Charles Robert Cockerell in his designs for the Bank of England (see **Bank of England, 1844**).

Palladio had become widely imitated in Britain, starting with the work of Inigo Jones, whose Banqueting House in Whitehall of 1619 is a masterful interpretation of Palladianism. The influence of Palladio's work on British architecture gained impetus in the 18th century as a result of the repeated publication of his collected works.

By the time of the great expansion of housing in places like London, Edinburgh and Bath in the 18th century, the Palladian design was nearly always used, but by the middle of the 19th century, engaged as this was in the **battle of the styles**, Palladianism had declined.

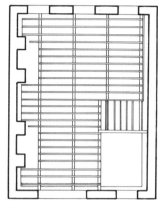

Upper-floor plan of a typical Georgian house, showing the network of timber that supported the floors and helped tie the building together.

columns, or pediments: the façade is just a stone wall with a carefully proportioned grid of windows, and very subtly placed horizontal bands, which evoke – quite consciously – the Renaissance and classical roots of the design. We are looking at what has become known as the Georgian period of architecture.

Despite this sophisticated architectural ancestry, the Georgian terraced house was a very basic piece of construction, judged by later standards. Materials would generally be of local origin: if stone was available, all well and good; if only clay could be obtained, then bricks would be baked 'on site'.

Internally, the houses would be divided into small rooms; partly because each used primitive methods for heating and lighting, but also because the walls all helped to support each other, and because it was economical to purchase in short lengths only the timber used for the floors.

When moulded decoration was used, it was made by hand on site. Although Birkenhead had the benefit of being close to a major river, transportation of building materials was still generally rudimentary. It is worth noting that in 1830, while Hamilton Square was under construction, the world's first purpose-built railway station opened on the Liverpool–Manchester Railway, just across the Mersey.

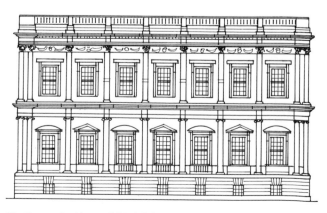

The Banqueting House, Whitehall: Inigo Jones, 1619.

Brunswick Buildings, Liverpool: A. & G. Williams, 1841.

Aedicule: simply applied classical ornamentation around a window in a terraced house of 1857 in Camberwell, London. It turns the window into a little 'building'.

103 Princess Street, Manchester (the former Mechanics Institute): J Gregan, 1854.

The palazzo

The palazzo model had been favoured in housing design since the early 18th century, but it was also adapted for the design of institutional and commercial buildings. Following studies in Italy, Charles Barry had designed the Travellers Club and the next-door Reform Club in Pall Mall, in 1829 and 1837 respectively, and these two influential buildings established the palazzo model as being different, liberal and – most of all – flattering, through its associations with Renaissance wealth.

The palazzo was an especially suitable style for the newly emerging commercial buildings of Britain as its details were easy to apply to the façade of a large building, which would otherwise have looked like a plain box, since the palazzo did not require ornamental porches or colonnades. Brunswick Buildings in Liverpool were the first such construction to use the new idiom.

In basic composition the palazzo is typically classical, being divided into three horizontal zones – a base, a middle and a top – and each of these zones has its own different design of window. The lowest band at the base of the building appears to be the strongest, and its windows are usually small, set in very thick-looking rusticated walls. The middle band of windows is the grandest, and these are surrounded by ornamentation. In Italian palazzos this part of the building was called the *piano nobile* (or principal floor), which contained the palace's main reception rooms. The degree of ornamentation, with a pair of columns on either side and a pediment above, often makes each window look like a little building in its own right.

At the Banqueting House by Inigo Jones (1619) the window pediments alternate between being triangular and curved. This use of the image of little 'buildings' or aedicules is a major element in the classical 'language' of architecture.

Battle of the styles
See Manchester Town Hall, 1868
Portico/Temple front
See Classical architecture, in Bank of England, 1844

Bank of England, Bristol 1844

In the 1840s, by the time Charles Robert Cockeroll designed the three provincial branches of the Bank of England in Bristol, Liverpool and Manchester, the strict rules of **classical architecture** were becoming difficult to apply to commercial premises like banks. These institutions were beginning to prosper, and often had to be squeezed onto tight inner-city sites. The Bristol bank in particular occupies a very narrow plot on a narrow street.

As a consequence, banks had to be built high, and their windows also had to be as large as possible so as to illuminate the banking hall and offices inside. Increasing the size of the windows was the only solution to getting enough light: gas only really started to establish itself as an alternative source of light to oil and candles in the second half of the century, and electricity did not start to compete with gas in towns until the 1890s.

Cockerell's designs are very inventive in adapting the classical rules to deal with these problems, for the rules were in truth not really suited to narrow and tall buildings, with large windows. He was well acquainted with classical architecture, belonging as he did to that generation of young men that went on 'grand tours' of the Greek and Roman antiquities. In his case, it was an exceptionally long tour, lasting until he was 29 years old.

Like that of the other two branches, Cockerell's design for the Bristol bank mixes what he saw on the tour in a way that was new, and quite acceptable to the mid-19th century.

The main motif of the façade is a three-bay colonnade of Doric columns. To the Victorian mind the Doric order was associated with strength and security, which was entirely appropriate for a bank. The design of these columns, with the horizontal entablature that stands on them, is a scholarly use of classical Greek architecture. But no Greek building could serve as a model for Cockerell to copy for a bank that needed to be so tall and so thin. To solve the problem, he placed another storey on top of the Greek colonnade, but this time using arched windows deriving, if anywhere, from classical Rome. And above these windows he placed a large triangular pediment. So, in effect he had lifted the pediment by a whole storey from its conventional position, completely breaking the classical rules, yet at the same time producing a very satisfying architectural composition.

Between the major features of the façade – the columns and the arches – Cockerell crammed as much

Development of the façade of Andrea Palladio's S. Giorgio Maggiore in Venice, 1565, which also used classical forms to solve an unclassical problem. this time, how to put a portico onto the façade of a conventional church, with its high central nave and side aisles: Palladio took a tall portico (a), a wide one (b), and then put the two together (c).

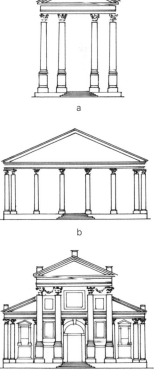

The façade of the Bank of England, Liverpool 1848.

window space as propriety could allow, thus getting as much light as possible into the banking hall behind.

But the quality of the Bristol bank lies not just in the way it stretched the rules by the insertion of an additional storey; it is also carefully thought out in even the subtlest of its details. For instance, it is set back from the line of the adjacent buildings by not quite a metre, but doing so has made it appear much more imposing on the narrow street. This recess is emphasized by the strong-looking rusticated walls that protrude from both ends of the frontage. Even the wall around the upper arched windows is set back from the wall surface beneath it, giving an impression of yet more depth. It is extraordinary how much modelling – both real and implied – has been achieved in such a restricted site.

Cockerell's Bank of England branch in Liverpool 'stretches' classical architecture in a very similar way, and is even grander than the Bristol branch. It is more fortunately positioned, standing at the end of a long vista up Brunswick Street.

Cockerell's banks are a demonstration of how flexible the classical style of architecture could be when it was employed by a capable exponent. But the popularity of temple fronts and colonnades for commercial architecture soon declined, to be taken over by the much more adaptable **palazzo** model, and later in the century by the even more flexible Gothic idiom.

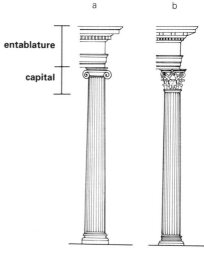

Sir William Chambers's analysis of (a) the Ionic and (b) the Corinthian orders.

Classical architecture

An understanding of the architecture of classical Greece and Rome has provided the basis for European architecture for the last 2000 years. Over this time its qualities have sometimes been interpreted very flexibly; at others it has been copied in the minutest detail. The palazzo design of **Hamilton Square, 1830** was a liberal reinterpretation of classical architecture, while the Bank of England at Bristol was more scholarly.

At its most fundamental, classical architecture requires a building's exterior to be composed so that it looks as if it has a strong base, a well-defined middle and a roof. In this way the building appears to be well constructed and able to provide adequate shelter.

Classicism also requires a building to have a recognizable face, or façade, in the same way that people have faces. The façade is the most important part of the building's exterior, and is often the point where the entrance is. Furthermore, a classical building should be composed so that it is symmetrical on either side of the vertical axis, which passes through the centre of the façade.

The basic qualities of classical architecture have never been forgotten in British urban building, although the interpretation of details has been very wide indeed. When it originated in the Middle Ages, even Gothic architecture, which we will soon see re-emerging a little later in the 19th century, was close in many respects to the architecture of classical Greece and Rome – what differed were the details. The most fundamental element of classical composition is the portico, or the front of a classical temple, which

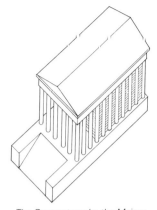

The Roman temple: the Maison Carrée at Nîmes, AD 120. It has a base, a middle part and a roof, and is perfectly symmetrical. Birmingham Town Hall, built in 1832, is very similar.

The Doric order: the portico of the Temple of Apollo Epicurius, Greece, 430 BC.

The Corinthian order on the upper part of the portico of St George's Hall, Liverpool, started in 1841 (C. R. Cockerell helped to design it).

St Vincent Street Church, Glasgow: Alexander 'Greek' Thomson, 1857.

Gothic
See All Saints, Margaret St, 1855
Modern architecture
See Wicklands Avenue, 1934
Office buildings
See p. 5, top illustration; Oriel Chambers, 1864; Lion Chambers, 1905; Willis, Faber & Dumas, 1975; Hillingdon Civic Centre, 1977; Crown Offices, 1980; Canary Wharf, 1990
Palazzo
See Hamilton Square, 1830

combines the fundamental features of a base, middle and a top, as well as being composed symmetrically into a façade. It has become the most enduring image of a building that there ever has been in British architecture. This 'temple' form was supposed to be derived from primitive architecture, and scholars of Cockerell's time produced fanciful drawings of ancient huts covered in twigs in an attempt to argue for classical architecture's universal application. Although the portico, with its base, columns and triangular pediment, has a powerful simplicity, there was a rich variety in the ways its details could be designed. These details were elaborate, and very seriously studied by architectural scholars. They centred around the use of columns and beams, whose size, spacing and exact design had been refined to perfection by the Greeks and Romans, who had grouped the designs into key variations that became known as the 'orders'. Using the orders, an architect could choose between the plain Tuscan, the graceful Doric, the slender Ionic, with its 'volute' capital, or the decorative Corinthian, with its ornate capital of acanthus leaves. When designing buildings with many floors, the classical architect would naturally choose a heavy, strong order like the Tuscan for the lowest storey, and a lighter order like the Ionic or Corinthian for the top.

In the 19th century different orders were selected because of their appropriateness to the function of the building. A bank, which needed to appear secure and strong, would use a stout order like the Doric, as in the Bank of England branch at Bristol. But a theatre, or a gentlemen's club, would be more likely to use one of the more ornate orders, and the Ionic was thought to be particularly delicate.

As we will see, attitudes towards the classical language of architecture varied throughout the 19th and 20th centuries. In the early 19th century there was a strong classical revival, during which many important public buildings like the British Museum, or St George's Hall, Liverpool, were designed as powerful and scholarly compositions of columns and pediments. But the century is more marked by its creative reinterpretation of the classical language, of which Cockerell's banks are just one example, and we should not forget the work of Alexander 'Greek' Thomson, whose Glasgow churches of the 1850s were highly original. This fascination with the re-use of Greek and Roman architecture had its most recent, rather humourless fling in the early 20th century (see **Selfridges, 1907**), before architects became preoccupied with the temporary attraction of something altogether more **Modern**.

Albert Dock, Liverpool 1845

Cast and wrought iron

Builders have known about iron for thousands of years, even if its use was only very restricted, due to the difficulties in its manufacture.

To obtain iron, iron ore has to be melted to some 1500°C, at which point molten iron runs out. The molten iron is then poured into simple bar shapes called 'pigs'. Getting to that temperature requires much fuel: originally wood was used, then coal, and after 1709, when Abraham Darby invented it, coke.

Cast iron was made by reheating the pig iron and pouring it into moulds. These moulds would usually be made by pressing a wooden pattern into sand, which meant that only a limited range of shapes could be cast. The first iron bridge was built in Coalbrookdale in 1779, and by 1845 cast iron had been used in the Kew Palmhouse, with its span of 32 m.

But due to impurities within it, cast iron is very weak in tension. It cannot be pulled, stretched or bent, or else it snaps or shatters. In 1848 the cast-iron Tay Bridge collapsed when a train full of passengers was crossing it, and from then onwards the material's use in building structure declined, especially for bridges, which have to suffer very high tensile forces.

Wrought iron consequently gained in popularity. 'Wrought' is the old English version of the word 'worked': hence wrought iron is 'worked' or forged with a hammer, knocking out the metal's impurities, so that it can cope with tension as well as compression. Wrought iron is more expensive to produce, but is lighter than cast iron.

Iron has also enjoyed great popularity as a decorative material, and it is interesting that cast iron gradually took over from wrought iron as the more popular medium. Before the 19th century the blacksmith's job was to 'work' iron into architectural decoration, but this was labour-intensive, 'one-off' work. By the time the great housing estates were being developed in the late 18th century, their builders turned to cast iron for decorative elements like balcony railings, simply because the same moulds could be used time after time (see the opening photograph of **Hamilton Square, 1830**). By the middle of the 19th century, cast-iron decoration had become big business, advertised in catalogues and with nationwide distribution.

The popularity of cast-iron decoration declined in the 1880s, and has not yet returned, although there is a good market in **glass-reinforced plastic** imitations of cast-iron decoration.

The imposing Albert Dock in Liverpool, designed by Jesse Hartley, brought together two of the latest ideas of the time in warehouse construction.

One was the concept of the 'enclosed' warehouse system, in which a whole square of buildings was designed to face inwards towards the dock. This enabled goods to be unloaded straight from the ships into the warehouses, and it also prevented thieving, since access to the waterside was restricted. St Katherine's Dock warehouse, next to the Tower of London, had been designed by Philip Hardwick ten years earlier, and had pioneered the enclosed design. It was the first warehouse to be built right at the water's edge, to allow for easy handling of cargoes from ship to secure storage.

The other innovation at Albert Dock was its form of construction, which, being entirely out of brick and **cast iron**, made it completely fireproof. Timber had been used in the floor construction of St Katherine's Dock, but since the mid-18th century, when large textile mills were built using timber, fire had been a very real risk.

The Liverpool Warehouse Act of 1843 introduced a system of registering warehouses according to how fireproof they were. Those built entirely of brick and iron would be offered reduced insurance premiums. So, despite his original intention of using timber flooring, Hartley was persuaded to adopt the fully fireproof system.

The vast new warehouses were to rise 20 m in five full storeys above the dock edge, with a basement below. Although the external walls are built of brick, the entire interior is supported on a framework of iron columns and beams. The cast-iron columns form rectangular 'bays' about 5 m long by 3 m wide, and at each floor level a cast-iron beam spans the longer distance between the columns. Bricks were laid in shallow vaults between these beams, forming a gently undulating 'ceiling' that is both very strong, and fireproof. A concrete floor filling was then laid on the top surface of the brick vaults, to provide a smooth floor for the storey above. This technique of spanning brick arches between iron beams had been developed in France in the middle of the 18th century, and is known as 'Jack-arch' construction.

Apart from their innovation in design, the Albert Dock warehouses are breathtaking for their sheer size, and for the simple clarity of their design. They almost completely surround the dock, and their façades are totally uniform. They could be said to be in a classical

The cast-iron Kew Palmhouse: Decimus Burton and Richard Turner, 1845.

idiom of engineering – not scholarly, but asserting the basic qualities of **classicism**. At the dock's edge the ground floor of each warehouse is open, with only a colonnade of vast iron columns supporting the walls above. At regular intervals there are arches for cranes, and there are just enough of these to enliven the façades and stop them from becoming monotonous. The only other features on the façades are the orderly rows of windows and loading doors.

Albert Dock's architectural qualities were not always apparent. Sir James Picton, writing in his *Memorials of Liverpool* of 1873, said: 'It is to be regretted that no attention whatsoever has been paid to beauty as well as strength. The enormous pile of warehouses ... is simply a hideous pile of naked brickwork.'

In the north-west corner of the dock is the Dock Office – a separate building designed by Hardwick, but with another storey added to the design by Hartley (the two had collaborated on the design of the warehouses). The Dock Office has a massive

View of Albert Dock towards the Pier Head. The range of warehouses on the left is now the Tate of the North gallery; that on the right is the Maritime Museum.

classical portico with four plain columns supporting an entablature and pediment. The entire portico is built of cast iron.

Hartley was very thorough with his design work. He had been trained as a stone mason in Yorkshire, but had also worked in an architectural office. He was devoted to his work, and more especially to saving money for his employers, the Liverpool Dock Committee, whom he served for 35 years. He had built extensive models of the Albert Dock to test its ability to withstand fire, and had opened an entire quarry in Scotland with a little coasting ship to supply the docks with granite.

While Hartley's architecture at Albert Dock is simple and immensely powerful, he employs a more decorative style elsewhere on the dock estate. His giant hydraulic accumulator tower at the entrance to Canada Dock inspired Picton to write: 'Whatever may have been the merits of Mr Jesse Hartley as an engineer – and they are undoubtedly great – a feeling for the beautiful was not one of them.'

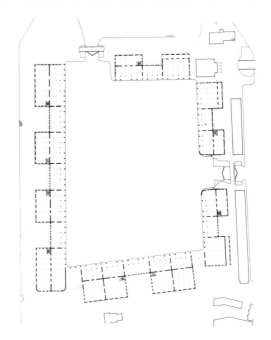

Plan of Albert Dock.

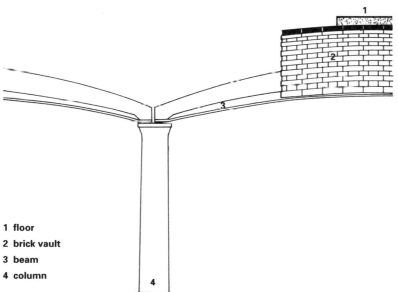
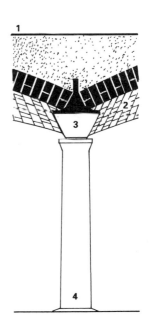

1 floor
2 brick vault
3 beam
4 column

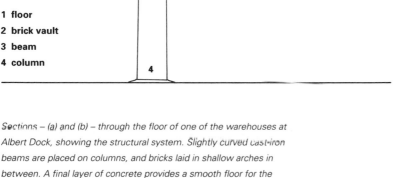

Sections – (a) and (b) – through the floor of one of the warehouses at Albert Dock, showing the structural system. Slightly curved cast-iron beams are placed on columns, and bricks laid in shallow arches in between. A final layer of concrete provides a smooth floor for the storey above.

Classicism
See Bank of England, 1844
Glass-reinforced plastic
See Herman Miller, 1977

Newcastle Central Station 1850

The scale of the mania for building railways in the 1840s is difficult for us to comprehend today. In Newcastle the arrival of the York, Newcastle and Berwick Railway in 1850 involved the broaching of the castle's walls and the construction of a magnificent high-level bridge over the Tyne that at last made an effective link with the neighbouring community in Gateshead.

Newcastle Central Station is no less audacious in its construction: its huge train shed was made up of three giant iron **spans**, placed side by side. Designed by the architect John Dobson in collaboration with the engineer Robert Stephenson, it was the first of the really great station sheds in Britain.

Dobson was an expert in many fields, and he invented the industrial process for rolling the malleable iron ribs that form these three great vaults over the platforms. He also devised a structural system that kept the number of columns at concourse level to a minimum, by placing a column only under every third of the curved roof ribs. The load of the intermediate ribs was taken up by a beam spanning the columns. This system was later used in Paddington and York stations. York (finished in 1877) shares with Newcastle the distinction of being built over a curve in the tracks, increasing the dramatic effect of the huge spans.

While Newcastle Station's train shed is constructed with a comparatively thin iron skeleton, its outer walls are built from stone, and are finished using a grand and 'correct' classical treatment. There was much scope for an extravagant external gesture because,

Exterior of Newcastle Central Station.

Large spans in iron and steel

Unlike today's railway stations, into which electric trains can purr silently and cleanly, their 19th-century counterparts, filled with smoke and steam, needed high roofs, which in turn required a new technology. Great stone buildings like the Pantheon in Rome, or Hagia Sophia in Istanbul, had managed to achieve spans of between 30 and 40 m. Railway stations did not need greater spans than this: what they did need, however, was that their roofs should be as lightweight as possible, so that they could sit on columns to allow trains and people to pass beneath; to let in as much daylight as possible; and to provide enough space for all the smoke to rise above the platforms.

The three spans at Newcastle are each 60 m wide, but this figure was soon to be dramatically overtaken by the huge shed at St Pancras Station, London, of 1863, whose wrought-iron lattice ribs span 74 m.

As at Newcastle, the outward thrust from the St Pancras roof is counteracted by tension members that tie together the bases of each arch. At Newcastle these are in the form of thin rods up in the roof, but at St Pancras they are girders that run underneath the station floor and provide a base for the trains to run on. Considering the comparatively crude techniques in structural calculation that were available at the time to the designer of

St Pancras Station, William Henry Barlow, the shed is a triumph of engineering. It remained the widest span in the world until it was surpassed by the Galerie des Machines at the Paris Exhibition of 1889, which spanned a clear 114 m. This spectacular building pioneered the use of structural steel, and was designed using the principle of the three-pinned arch. At the apex the two sections of each truss were just joined by a pin; and at their base each truss was fixed to the ground with a hinged joint. At the time it caused some concern that such an immense load should meet the ground at such a small point, and it has been argued that the Galerie des Machines played a very important role in establishing the aesthetic that would eventually become Modern architecture in the 20th century.

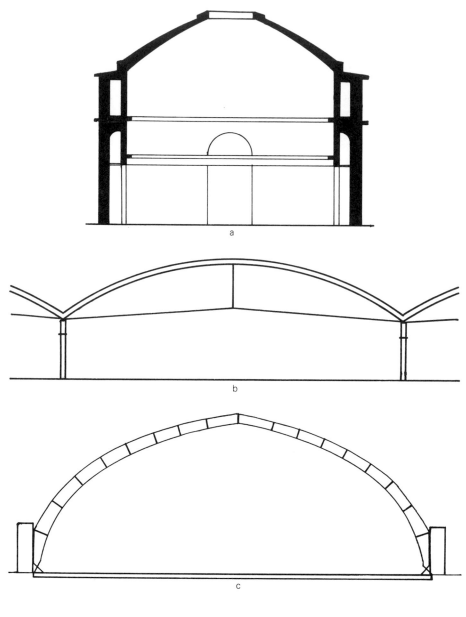

(a) the Pantheon, Rome, AD 123 (stone and brick); (b) Newcastle Central Station, 1848 (iron) – the tension members that keep the arches from spreading apart are shown beneath the main arch; (c) St Pancras Station, London, 1863 (iron) – here the tension members are underneath the railway tracks; (d) Galerie des Machines, Paris, 1889 (steel). (Illustrations not to same scale.)

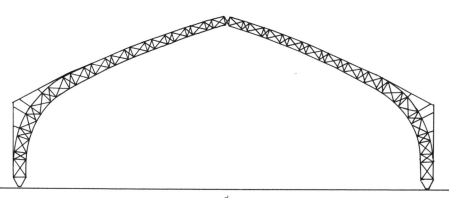

unlike at London's King's Cross, where the main station entrance is situated at the end of the tracks and is therefore rather narrow, at Newcastle the main entrance is beside the tracks, providing the opportunity to make a long entrance building.

During these pioneering days of the railways it was not unknown for there to be financial crises, and travellers were reassured by a substantial architectural rendition of a station's exterior, displaying the company's stability and strength. In 1848 the sponsors of Newcastle Station suffered a collapse in public confidence in their finances, and the original design for the entrance block had to be pared down to meet a lower budget.

Dobson's original intention was to provide an open colonnade that would have made the station one of the finest neoclassical buildings in Europe. A surviving print shows an immensely impressive design, with a grand colonnade of paired Doric columns and arches in between, and a large central portico with seated carved figures on top. It was Roman in inspiration, and this style was becoming more favoured by railway developers than the more austere Greek classicism of, say, St George's Hall in Liverpool.

But the financial troubles, and a decision by the York, Newcastle and Berwick Railway to move its headquarters to Newcastle from York, and to requisition some of the façade as office space, meant that a rethink was needed. The scheme that was finally adopted was a poorer version of Dobson's original design. It was eventually carried out under the direction of Thomas Prosser (who later designed York Station), who used the classical vocabulary of architecture in a much less emphatic way than Dobson had intended.

Despite these changes, Newcastle Station demonstrates just how much money was spent on making the early railways architecturally acceptable. Put another way, the money spent on the outer buildings was a form of advertising. The *porte-cochère* at the front of the building turns the mundane experience of getting on a train into that of arriving at a sumptuous hotel. The early railways were desparate to be seen to be accepted by the societies among which they were built, and the expense they lavished on their architecture proves it.

The train shed at St Pancras Station, London 1863.

All Saints, Margaret St, London 1855

This multicoloured brick church, designed by William Butterfield for a dense inner-London setting, helped to establish the precedent for urban Gothic architecture that was to survive until the end of the 19th century.

The construction of All Saints was partly in response to the gradual erosion of the status of the established Anglican Church in the early years of the century. It was not moving with the times, and the building of All Saints was promoted by a vigorous wing within the Church as a strong reassertion of the Church's power. Such an assertion also needed to be expressed by an architecture that was appropriately strong.

Despite the reduction of the Church's status, the State recognized how much it needed a strong religious influence to exert control over society. In the first half of the 19th century there had been a rapidly increasing urban population, which from time to time flexed its muscle and challenged the establishment. As early as 1819 a huge grant of £1 million of public money had been made available for the construction of inner-city churches with the express purpose of 'civilizing' the population – or, put another way, keeping the population under control.

These were known as Commissioners' churches, after the commission that allocated funds for construction. A further grant of £500 000 was made in 1825, and in the late 1840s, when All Saints was conceived, the risk of popular dissent was still acutely felt.

The Commissioners' churches were built in a variety of historical styles. Some were **classical** and some were **Gothic**. Gothic means, broadly, the architecture

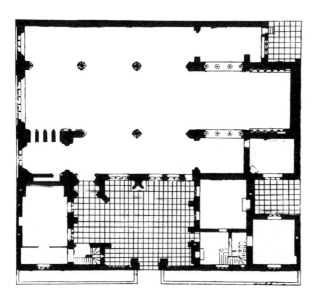

Plan of All Saints, Margaret Street (after the Builder), 1853.

Gothic

Gothic architecture was developed in the great cathedrals of northern Europe from the 11th century onwards. The master masons who designed these immense structures tried to build ever upwards, and to make the vast church interiors as well lit as possible, developing techniques by trial and error that might enable them to do away with as much of the stone walls as possible and turn them into screens of glass.

To do this, they channelled the huge weight of the stone vaults above the nave down on to points in the side walls, by using stone ribs within the vault. The side walls, which no longer had to carry the weight of the vault continuously along their length, could now be pierced by large windows. From the inside, this enabled the cathedrals to look as if they were being held up by the thinnest of strips of stone. But on the outside, these thin strips had to be supported by stone buttresses coming out of the sides of the building. Even then, ways were found to pierce these buttresses, leaving only the most necessary parts of the structure; hence the name 'flying buttress', for there was more 'hole' than there was stone.

With this system the load from the upper parts is not just carried straight down to the ground. It is also carried outwards, through the flying buttress to the outer pier, which needs to be weighted down by the pinnacle above. It might look like mere decoration, but the Gothic system was, when it was devised, intensely logical.

By the beginning of the 13th century, the design of Gothic cathedrals had become essays in beauty using the minimum of materials, and this 'rational' architecture was greatly admired during the 19th century, which was searching for a characteristic architecture of its own.

By the early 16th century Gothic architecture had become more decorative: the late period of Gothic of Henry VII's Chapel at Westminster is more about covering every available surface with ribs and arches than it is about structural gymnastics.

Following the Gothic period, which lasted some 400 years in Britain, 19th-century designers turned their attention to what had been happening in the Italian **Renaissance**.

of the Middle Ages, but at the time when the Commissioners' churches were being introduced, few buildings really represented a scholarly approach to that style: they did not bother about being archaeologically perfect.

By the time that All Saints was being designed, the Gothic style was being taken very seriously. An ex-pharmacist and eccentric architect called Thomas Rickman had published a treatise as long ago as 1817 that had tried to trace the real history of English medieval church building. By the 1840s the construction of the Houses of Parliament had established the importance of the Gothic style for the whole nation to see. A. W. N. Pugin, who had collaborated on their design, wrote that the only truly Christian architecture was Gothic. Its attractions were that it was essentially northern European in origin; it was a very rational type of architecture – an architecture in which everything seemed to be there for a purpose, as opposed to frivolous decoration; and the 19th-century mind was attracted to the Gothic style because it romantically believed that it evoked a period when all members of society were supposed to be happy with their lot, and all were equally devoted to their Church. John Betjeman wrote in his book on architecture *Ghastly Good Taste* (1933) that the Gothic style reminded the Victorians of 'those happy days, when a man did not have a mind of his own, the king ruled the baron, the baron the yeoman, the yeoman the serf, and the Church ruled all.'

The version of the Gothic style that was taken as the starting point of the All Saints design was the so-called 'second pointed' or 'decorated' (the terms were

The Gothic system: the weight of the stone vault is channelled along ribs to points in the wall, which gradually evolved into no more than a row of columns. The outward thrust is resisted from the outside by flying buttresses.

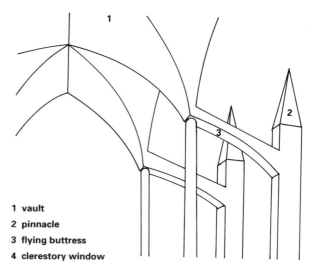

1 **vault**

2 **pinnacle**

3 **flying buttress**

4 **clerestory window**

19th-century concoctions). Examples of this are the nave of Lichfield Cathedral (1280) and the choir of Ely Cathedral (1350). These styles, which had evolved in the 14th century, were thought to be specifically English, and marked the most sophisticated achievement of Gothic architecture before it became more of a decorative style in the following century. The 19th-century theory was that the architect only had to study these medieval precedents to be able to invent a new 19th-century style – which was exactly what happened at Margaret Street.

All Saints also introduced a very significant new development – polychromy (or the use of many colours). Scholars were beginning to take an interest in colour generally. New technology was developing coloured printing in books and magazines; and a much wider range of **bricks** of all types was available for distribution around the country by railway. At Margaret Street it was also felt to be morally correct if the colour on buildings was not just painted on, or skin-deep, but was actually part of the building's structure, in the same way that a geological section will highlight the actual structure of a landscape. All Saints is faced (so it is still a bit of an illusion) with red and black bricks, with stone dressings. But the bricks were by no means cheap, and their use was an emphatic break from the Georgian tradition of building in stone.

The result was an intensely vigorous piece of architecture, which was a very effective advertisement for the High Church Anglicans who built it, and it became the starting point for the High Victorian phase of the Gothic revival.

Reims Cathedral: exterior of the nave.

Reims Cathedral: the nave, c.1250.

Section through a typical Gothic church, showing the flying buttresses.

Bricks
For an account of the new developments in brick manufacture in the 19th century, see The Granary, 1869
Classical architecture
See Hamilton Square, 1830 and Bank of England, 1844
Renaissance
See Hamilton Square, 1830

Akroydon, Halifax 1861

There was nothing new about the building of self-sufficient communities according to visionary plans. The usual basis for these developments was religious. In the 18th century the Moravians, a German-based Protestant group, created a number of 'model communities' throughout Britain and the rest of the world, in which people came together to live, work and worship in a kind of utopia on earth.

But at the end of that century Robert Owen developed the factory-based community at New Lanark for commercial reasons, providing a whole range of social facilities in order to contain and civilize the community, as well as make it more profitable. This **philanthropic** idea formed the basis of a number of new communities that were founded in the middle of the century by wealthy industrialists. Sir Titus Salt, the worsted manufacturer, founded Saltaire just outside the grime of Bradford in 1850, in which 560 workers' houses were grouped around the imposing mill.

The carpet tycoon and Tory MP Colonel Edward Akroyd opened his mill in Halifax in 1836 and, following a previous experiment in housing at Copley, he started building his community, which he called Akroydon, in a suburb outside the town.

The most conspicuous feature of Akroydon is the huge church of All Souls, which was designed by Sir George Gilbert Scott, who considered it the best of the many churches he had designed. Nearby stands a statue of the good colonel, which was completed in his lifetime. The inhabitants were to be made aware of their earthly benefactor standing second only to God. Like Titus Salt, Akroyd did not seek anonymity.

It was in these industrialists' interests to provide housing for their employees: rents were easily collected as deductions from wages; and because it was so simple to evict people from their homes, they generally became subservient to their landlords. There was also good business sense in such ventures: at Akroydon there was a return of 6 per cent each year from the initial outlay required to build the scheme.

Scott was originally put in charge of planning the development. He formed a central grassed square with a Gothic 'cross' in the middle, and around the square the workers' houses were built in neat, orderly rows. Today the impression is one of great tranquillity. The roads alternate with back alleys, and there are none of the unpopular **back-to-back houses**. The grid-iron of streets is occasionally crossed by a narrow alleyway, or snicket. Every house has its own backyard and privy.

Philanthropic organizations

The development of what is now termed 'social housing' can be traced through the early schemes at Saltaire, Akroydon and West Hill Park. These paternalistic settlements were built for the benefit of specific groups of employees, but the first organizations to deal in a systematic way with the housing problem in general were the philanthropic organizations, which were set up on a commercial basis in the second half of the 19th century.

Capital was raised on the assurance of a steady return on the investment; the houses were built, and the return on the investment came from the rents received from the tenants. The biggest philanthropic organizations were established by industrialists like George Peabody, the American merchant, who in 1862 gave an initial gift of £150 000 to start building multi-storey tenement blocks. The following year Sydney Waterlow founded the Improved Industrial Dwellings Society, which paid a dividend of 5 per cent to those who had invested in it.

Waterlow strongly believed that the housing should not be provided for the poorest members of society, but for those 'most worth working for' – the industrious artisans. And then, he believed, the 'lower orders, who are least likely to appreciate the comforts of a decent home' would be able to move up into the homes that the artisans had just vacated.

There was always a moral dimension to philanthropic housing: the working classes who were given homes by the organizations were supposed, in return, to be sober and industrious. It was, in effect, a means of control – houses in exchange for social compliance.

The concept of local government emerged out of the old parish councils at the end of the 19th century, and it took on much of the badly needed responsibility for housing (see **Boundary Street Estate, 1895**). But the aura of patronage has never really disappeared: until only recently local councillors in some areas have retained the right to nominate people whom they deem fit to be rehoused, and in the last years of the 20th century the **community architecture** movement never really challenged who holds the power.

The amount of architectural embellishment increases with the status of the people who lived in the houses. The humblest dwellings are virtually unadorned, while higher-class houses are given the symbols of status – bay windows and an increasing degree of ornamentation in the **Gothic** style. The use of this style was imagined by Scott to be a way of educating the people, although at the time of construction the workers thought the Gothic gables made the buildings look a little bit too much like almshouses.

Akroyd's great rival in Halifax was John Crossley, another carpet tycoon. They had argued over plans for a new town hall: Akroyd had wanted a Gothic structure on the edge of town, but Crossley won, and a classical town hall, designed by Sir Charles Barry, was built in 1859.

Crossley built the neighbouring development of West Hill Park almost immediately after Akroydon. Here again, there was a strict grading of the dwellings by class. But West Hill Park introduced another typically Victorian idea, that all the houses should be

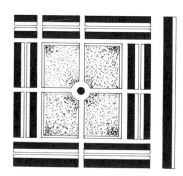

The schematic plan of Akroydon around the grassed square, with the Gothic monument in the centre.

The Victorian Gothic monument in the grass square at the heart of Akroydon.

zoned according to class and, in the words of the architect's brief, positioned so as 'to limit the look-out from each class of house, to cottages of a similar, and not inferior, character'.

Saltaire and Akroydon were followed by industrial estates at Bournville in Birmingham for Cadbury's chocolate-factory workers (1879), and Port Sunlight in Cheshire for Lever's soap factory (1888).

Early philanthropic flats: Verandah Cottages, North Hill, Highgate, erected in 1863 'for the benefit of the Industrial Classes'.

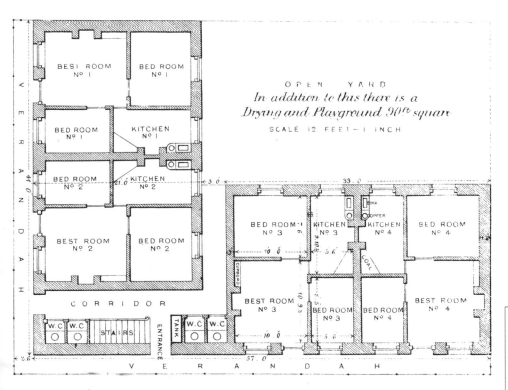

VERANDAH COTTAGES (REGISTERED) NORTH HILL, HIGHGATE, N.
(ERECTED FOR THE BENEFIT OF THE INDUSTRIAL CLASSES)
Designed & Executed by Mr C. Wood, Builder, Laurel Cottage, Highgate; for the Proprietor 1863.

Oriel Chambers, Liverpool 1864

Oriel Chambers in Liverpool is interesting because its significance was only recognized many decades after it was completed in 1864, and after it had virtually ruined the reputation of its architect, Peter Ellis.

It was built as an **office** block, which as a building type was still fairly new at the time. The first known modern office block had been built in the same city 20 years earlier: Brunswick Buildings of 1843 had been one of the first commercial buildings to be modelled on an Italian palazzo. Oriel Chambers broke with this tradition in a startling way, and offered a stylistic approach that had no obvious historical precedent (although the word 'Oriel', used in its name, clearly refers to the medieval window type that covers its façade).

With hindsight it is hard to believe how the building could evoke such strong reactions when it was completed, but the critic for the *Builder* magazine was not impressed: 'The plainest brick warehouse in the town is infinitely superior as a building to that large agglomeration of protruding plate-glass bubbles . . . termed Oriel Chambers. Did we not see this vast abortion – which would be depressing were it not ludicrous – with our own eyes, we would have doubted the possibility of its existence.' This reaction did nothing to enhance Ellis's reputation, and apart from building another similar structure nearby a little later, his career as an architect declined, and he ended up working as an obscure civil engineer.

Oriel Chambers becomes significant in architectural history because it signals so many of the stylistic and constructional techniques that evolved into **Modern architecture** over half a century later. The main façade has stone mullions between the protruding 'bubbles' of **glass**, and these are treated, along with the gable at the top, to a kind of Gothic decoration. But the mullions do not constitute the building's main structure, which is in fact an internal **cast-iron** frame in which square stanchions support inverted T-beams, spanned by shallow 'jack-arched' brick floors. The technique is remarkably similar to that used at **Albert Dock, 1845** a little more than ten years earlier, and it is more than likely that the critic writing in the *Builder* had Albert Dock in mind when he spoke of the 'plainest brick warehouse'.

From the 1850s a tradition of using cast iron had been well established in Glasgow and in the USA. The most famous of the early Glasgow buildings is Gardners' warehouse, Jamaica Street, of 1855, designed by John Baird using an iron structural

Glass

In the 18th century glass was only available in very small sections, formed by spinning a hot globule of glass into a disc shape. The famous 'bullseye' windows of today's country teashops are a replica of the central section of the disc shape, which was the least attractive and cheapest part to produce.

A tax on glass was lifted in 1845, and by the same time new processes allowed much larger sheets a whole storey high to be made, thus enabling fully glazed shopfronts to be built. Large areas of glass did not meet with everyone's approval – we have seen the reception that critics gave to Oriel Chambers – and other influential commentators believed that the lowest part of a building should appear to be able to carry the weight of the upper parts. To them a transparent ground floor was irrational, because the weight was not carried by the wall, but by the deep beam that spanned the top of the glass.

Cast iron
See Albert Dock, 1845 and Newcastle Central Station, 1850
Curtain walling and modern architecture
See Pioneer Health Centre, 1935; Peter Jones, 1935; Willis, Faber & Dumas, 1975
Office buildings
See Bank of England, 1844, Lion Chambers, 1905; Willis, Faber & Dumas, 1975; Hillingdon Civic Centre, 1977; Crown Offices, 1980; Canary Wharf, 1990

Gardners, Glasgow, 1855.

system patented by R. McConnel. Despite its industrial construction, it is a very 'architectural' building, and great care has been taken in composing the façade and its details.

In the interior of Oriel Chambers there is no attempt to disguise the structure, and to the rear of the building the façade that faces the private courtyard is even more utilitarian: an almost completely glazed wall is cantilevered out from the cast-iron verticals, making it one of the earliest examples of **curtain walling**.

Ellis's two Liverpool buildings set us a problem – when they were built they were sufficiently unpopular to set his career on its downward slide. And yet, a full century after Oriel Chambers was completed, Quentin Hughes, in his book *Seaport* (1964), describes Ellis as a 'genius' who was 'much abused in his own day'.

Nikolaus Pevsner also admired the building, calling it 'one of the most remarkable of its date in Europe'. Like many other writers in the 1960s, both Hughes and Pevsner were apologists for the Modern movement. Their admiration for Oriel Chambers would have surprised poor Ellis, who was after all only using established engineering techniques in a *nouveau riche* port that had little regard for convention.

Close-up of the façade of Oriel Chambers.

Manchester Town Hall 1868

Bolton Town Hall: W. Hill, 1866.

Stockport Town Hall: A. B. Thomas, 1904.

From the 1830s onwards dramatic changes took place within local government. The Municipal Corporations Act of 1835 established the principle of councils being elected by rate-payers, although in those days 'rate-payer' meant a man with property. New corporations were formed – both Birmingham and Manchester were incorporated in 1838 – and they set about establishing large bureaucracies for themselves, which needed accommodation. The Birmingham and Manchester corporations both built new **town halls**, with space inside for a great chamber, mayoral rooms and administrative offices.

Birmingham Town Hall of 1835 still survives. It is a huge classical temple – rather like the Maison Carrée at Nîmes (see p. 19, top illustration) – clad in Anglesey marble, and standing on an arcaded plinth. It was designed by the eponymous inventor of the Hansom cab, and has been called England's best example of a Roman temple.

Built a little later, Leeds Town Hall of 1853 was also classical. Designed by Cuthbert Brodrick, it remains an imposing sight in the centre of the city, and was used as a model for many other new town halls, including the magnificent one at Bolton of 1866.

But in the middle decades of the 19th century the **battle of the styles** was raging mercilessly in the centres of civic power of the new cities. If it was won at all, the victor was Manchester Town Hall, which firmly established a picturesque, free interpretation of the Gothic idiom that was perfectly in keeping with pride in new-found commercial success.

Manchester's original town hall, which was built at the same time as Birmingham's, had proved inadequate, and in 1867 the city sponsored a competition for a new town hall. Civic affairs were expanding as rapidly as the prosperity of the city, and a new building was wanted that not only provided more office space, but that could also be a symbol of civic pride and opulence.

One hundred and thirty schemes were entered into the competition, and the words that some of their architects used to describe them show how important it was for new architectural designs to be based on historical styles: there was a 'perpendicular treatment of Venetian Gothic', a scheme that was 'free Italian from the French point of view', and another that was 'in the best period of French feudal architecture, considerably refined'.

The design that was eventually chosen was by the local architect Alfred Waterhouse, and it was

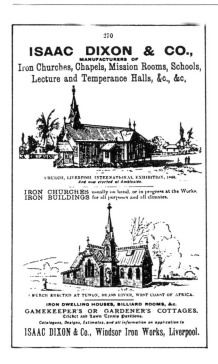

The prefabricated tin sheds that were shipped to the colonies to serve as schoolrooms and churches.

The battle of the styles

The mid-19th century saw the decline of the importance of **classical architecture**, which had dominated architectural thought since the Renaissance. It was no longer regarded as the only route by which civilization and perfection could be attained. With the new spirit of enlightenment and liberalism came the idea that civilization had flourished at other times, and in places other than Greece or Rome.

In Britain the newly emerging middle classes were not going to be content with the strictly codified rules of classicism. They wanted to assert themselves. They developed a hunger, not only for the architecture that they saw the aristocracy using, but also for any style that they felt inclined to choose. The antagonism between the groups of the cultural élite who espoused different styles in the middle of the 19th century was intense and complex. It is difficult to appreciate now how such matters came to be taken so seriously, yet the architectural establishment of today has its factions, just as it has always had.

By the middle of the century Gothic had come to be thought of by some as the only 'correct' style of architecture. Tories of the extreme right and the High Anglican Church in particular felt that Gothic was the national architecture: its motifs were re-created time and again in the 19th century to give a medieval (and therefore somehow pious) look to buildings, right down to the prefabricated tin sheds that were shipped overseas from the ports of Bristol and Liverpool to serve as schoolrooms and churches in the colonies of America and Australia.

In the 1850s the battle of the styles had raged over the design of the new Foreign Office in London. It was the subject of a competition in 1856, but the winning design was rejected by the Liberal prime minister, Lord Palmerston. Being closely associated with the Gothic style, the Tory party – which came back to power in 1858 – chose the architect Sir George Gilbert Scott's scheme because it was Gothic. But the Liberals were back in power again the following year, and even though Scott kept the job, he was put under pressure by Palmerston to change his Gothic scheme because it was associated with the Tories.

Apparently Scott then went out and 'bought some costly books on Italian architecture' in order to 'rub up' on his knowledge of that style, and in 1861 he produced the classical design that was eventually built.

But the appeal of Gothic was also felt by the strong commercial powers that had become established in the proud new industrial cities. To them the style symbolized freedom and democracy, and they associated it with national pride.

The 20th-century architectural historian Nikolaus Pevsner describes, a little disparagingly, the variety of building styles that emerged in the middle of the 19th century as the 'Fancy Dress Ball of Architecture'. It is true that, in comparison with the revolution in architecture that took place in the 20th century, the innovations of the 19th appear cosmetic. But this is the period when our great town centres evolved, and when the massive inner suburban expansions took place. Much of it survives – the Fancy Dress Ball is still with us, and it occupies a dominant place in our architectural inheritance.

Classical architecture
See Hamilton Square, 1830 and the Bank of England, 1844
Georgian architecture
See Hamilton Square, 1830
Town halls
Compare Manchester Town Hall with Hillingdon Civic Centre, 1977

described as '13th-century Gothic suffused with the feeling and spirit of the present age'. The Gothic idiom was considered to be democratic and English, and preferable to the classical idiom, which was deemed so class-ridden.

But the main reason for the choice of Waterhouse's scheme was its economical use of what was a very cramped site. Standing outside the main front of the Town Hall on Albert Square, it is difficult to appreciate the complexity of the design, but a look at the plan shows how ingenious it is. The main council chamber is in the middle, in its own structure, which is joined to the rest of the building only at the points of entrance. It is like a building within a building. This allows enough open space around the chamber to let daylight in through huge side windows.

The town hall offices surround the chamber, and are built to form a triangle, right up to the edges of the site. A long corridor runs round the inner face of these offices. At each of the three corners there is a spiral staircase off the corridor, while in addition two large formal staircases give access to the council chamber. The office windows face the outside and are graded in importance, starting with the mayor's office on the first floor facing Albert Square. Manchester Town Hall

established the Gothic idiom for civic buildings, and also helped to establish Waterhouse's reputation.

He later went on to design the hotel for Liverpool's Lime Street Station, and other town halls in Knutsford and Reading. He designed a number of branches for the Prudential Assurance Company, including one in London (1880), Liverpool (1886), Nottingham and Edinburgh (both 1895), creating for these a Gothic red-brick and **terracotta** architecture that was so much part of the late-19th-century commercial scene. Waterhouse also designed the Hotel Metropole in Brighton (1889) and his most famous commission of all, the Natural History Museum in London (1868).

At Manchester Town Hall he used Gothic to create a picturesque composition which, with its tower and bay windows and angle turrets, verges on the fantastic. But Waterhouse also exploited the freedom that the Gothic style could give – the freedom to plan an immensely efficient town hall for Manchester, while at the same time creating a powerful advertisement for the new city, which would bear favourable comparison with the rival cities of Liverpool, with its classical town hall originally designed by John Wood of Bath in 1749, and Leeds, with its massive and confident classical design of 1853.

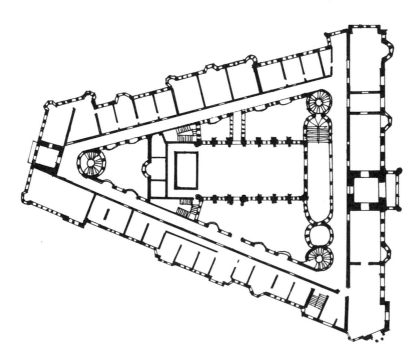

*Plan of Manchester Town Hall: the Council Chamber is the
rectangular structure in the centre.*

Terracotta

From the 1860s terracotta, literally 'baked earth', became a popular form of ornamental building material, due to its strength and relative cheapness. It was well suited to the Gothic and **Queen Anne revival** styles prevalent at this time.

It was not a new idea: even Coade Stone, patented in 1769, is technically a form of terracotta, but its use for ornamental work was restricted because of its high cost. But now, in the mid-19th century, with sophisticated manufacture and distribution, terracotta became commonplace on even the smallest buildings.

In the 19th century terracotta would have been moulded from high-alumina clays, often from the coal measures of the Midlands. These clays were ground into a fine paste, and then pressed into moulds to a thickness of about 25 mm, before being fired in kilns at a very high temperature. The colour of the final product could range from a honey yellow to a deep red. It was a high-technology production process for the time and required a great deal of care, especially as the shrinkage after firing tended to be irregular. In addition, occasional accidents in the kiln could make delivery times to building sites erratic. However, terracotta was extremely versatile, and its good weathering quality allowed it to be used in the most exposed locations. Price-wise it compared well with stone, but strength-wise it was thought to be better.

In the 1840s the Liverpool architect Edmund Sharpe built entire churches out of terracotta. They were commonly known as 'pot churches', since the terracotta units were generally hollow. Sharpe's intention had been to promote the use of terracotta made from clay from a local colliery, and everything in the churches, except the foundations and the rubble in the middle of the walls, was made from the material.

Despite criticism at the time, accusing it of being 'fake' ornament, terracotta rose in popularity, while the use of stucco as a form of ornament declined – another sign of the general trend away from labour-intensive 'on-site' methods towards high technology and national distribution.

In the 1860s terracotta was used on the first phase of the new Victoria and Albert Museum building, and its popularity peaked in the 1880s and 90s, when it was used extensively on new commercial buildings, especially in Manchester and Birmingham, as well as for schools and housing.

Queen Anne revival
See Primrose Hill School, 1885

The Granary, Bristol 1869

If Liverpool's **Albert Dock, 1846** is a warehouse structure with no pretensions towards the outside world,
then the Wait & James Granary in Bristol is the complete opposite. It is surrounded by public streets,
and commands them even today with its flamboyant
presence.

What is in fact a ten-storey stack of purely functional warehouse space has been faced with outer
walls of red **brick** with yellow trimmings, which
demonstrate both the great care that was taken in the
design and the wish of the building's original owners
to sponsor such design. The architects were Ponton &
Gough.

Unlike Albert Dock, the Granary's bricks are all
machine-made and, through careful specification,
formed into a range of pointed, round-topped, segmental and flat arches, such that no two storeys on the
façade are similar. The yellow bricks are used to a
much lesser extent within the arches, and run in horizontal bands at carefully chosen heights right round
the building.

Despite the huge bulk of the building, it still presents a satisfying overall composition through the use
of simple but effective architectural devices. As in a
palazzo, the lowest part appears to be the most massive: there is plenty of brickwork above the strong
pointed-arched openings (**Gothic** in style). Further up,
there are a variety of different arcades: in the middle
of the façade large arches run in front of two whole
floors, disguising the real internal organization of the
building. Yet the need for this arcade is obvious: it
looks almost like the *piano nobile* of an Italian palazzo,
and prevents the façade from becoming just a monotonous grid of openings. Within the arcades there is
more brickwork, perforated to allow for ventilation of
the interior. With each higher floor these brick screens
are set further back from the façade – a device that has
the effect of making the upper arcades look lighter and
airier than the lower ones. At the top of the building
there is – again in the fashion of a palazzo – a parapet
that is corbelled out from the wall surface and given
ornate battlements.

The Granary is impossible to categorize using conventional 19th-century labels. The building appears
almost disrespectful of architectural tradition, and it
has been said of one of its architects, W. V. Gough,
that 'it is hard to know whether to take Gough seriously as an architect: he was undoubtedly very short
of architectural tact, yet on occasion could bring off
a remarkable theatrical *tour de force*, whose very

Brick

The technique of firing clay
instead of drying it in the sun
has been known in Europe for
over 3000 years, and was
brought into Britain by the
Romans, many examples of
whose brickwork still survives.
A Roman brick was between
25 and 50 mm thick – much
thinner than the 65 mm brick
that we use today.
After the Romans had left
Britain, brick ceased to be
used until the early 14th
century, when it re-emerged in
the eastern counties of
England where local supplies
of timber and stone were
scarce and where there were
strong links with the Low
Countries, whose brick-
building tradition had
survived. After its re-
introduction, brick was still
an expensive material and
its manufacture was very
localized, the clay usually
being dug from the ground
near the building under
construction.
Brick clay was mixed with
water into a paste in a 'pug
mill', which, until the middle
of the 19th century, was
usually operated by muscle
power alone. Each brick was
then moulded by hand on a
table and allowed to dry. The
bricks were then collected into
piles, or 'clamps', and burnt,
using coal and ashes that had
been placed between the
bricks. Sometimes the ashes
were mixed into the paste
itself, causing a familiar blue-
black mottled effect on the
fired brick. This manufacturing
process took place near each
individual site until brick

production became more centralized in the 19th century. The use of local raw materials meant that early brickwork acquired strongly regional characteristics, often eradicated in later times by the builders' desire to display their ability to use the best, or the most expensive, materials. Colour is the most important aesthetic attribute of brick, and tastes in colour have changed dramatically over the years. In London, for example, yellow 'malms' or 'stocks' became popular at the beginning of the 19th century, replacing a fashion for red bricks, which were now thought to be too 'hot' in colour. By the end of the 19th century red bricks were back in vogue once the harder varieties had become available from north Wales. Then, returning full circle, the yellow stocks have regained popularity at the end of the 20th century, reflecting a desire to use building techniques that are 'traditional' and in keeping with the older built environment.

In earlier times there was a clearly understood hierarchy of brickwork, in which inferior types were used in hidden positions like fireplaces or partition walls. The next grade up would be used for the outside walls to the rear of the building. The front façade would employ the next grade from that, and the very best bricks would be reserved for arches, string courses and quoins, where display was expected. By the end of the 19th century up to 5 per cent

of the cost of building a house might be spent on special decorative bricks. (See also **Primrose Hill School, 1885** and **51–57 Ivydale Road, 1900**.) The construction of the railways, which helped to transport bricks around the country, played a vital role in the improvement of the quality and popularity of brickwork in the middle of the 19th century. In the 1850s railway interests had helped to promote the abolition of the brick tax, which had caused brick to decline in use throughout the previous century.

By the 1850s new techniques, including the development of powered grinding machines, which replaced the old muscle-powered pug mills, enabled harder clays from the Midlands and the North to be made into brick. Now it became possible to produce regular, smooth, hard bricks of consistent quality, even if – as in the case of **Fletton bricks** from around Peterborough – these were thought to look a little bland and vulgar.

The process of firing was also revolutionized. The walls of the train shed of St Pancras Station, built during the 1860s (see p. 19, illustration), were constructed in 'Gripper's bricks', named after Edward Gripper, an Essex farmer who moved to Nottingham in the 1850s. In 1867 he set up a large works for making his patented bricks under an exclusive licence to use the Hoffman kiln. This was a continuous-burning kiln invented in Germany in 1856, in which bricks were loaded,

Detail of the brickwork at the Granary.

burnt and cooled in a ring of chambers, the fire passing non-stop from one chamber to the next. It was considerably faster than the traditional method where the fire had to be allowed to burn itself out after each batch of bricks was made.

Mass production of bricks had arrived, and the new technology was also having an impact on architectural fashion. The new machine-made bricks, with their precise size and dazzling colours and vitreous glazes, captured the imagination. Wire-cut or pressed bricks, many from

Ruabon in north Wales, were becoming popular for use on the most prestigious parts of buildings.

The High Victorian Gothic phase of architecture, which became popular during the 1860s following the building of **All Saints, Margaret St, 1855**, was in part a celebration of polychromatic brickwork. The Gothic revival, with its use of intricate mouldings, encouraged a market in exquisite-shaped machine-made bricks, all of which could be ordered by catalogue and transported by train to any town in the country.

brashness was persuasive'.

But, as in other British 'boom' towns of the late 19th century, brashness was an architectural style. Templeton's Carpet Factory in Glasgow (designed by W. Leiper in 1889) is an even more colourful and self-assertive celebration of Victorian commerce. Both it and Ponton & Gough's Granary are in fact very serious attempts to give an architectural treatment to otherwise bland stacks of internal floors.

At about the time that Templeton's was being built, American architects were also turning their attention to the same problem, but on an even huger scale. The Marshall Field Wholesale Ware-house in Chicago of 1885 (H. H. Richardson) reinterprets the Palladian base and cornice, and unites internal floors with arcades of varying height in much the same way as in the Granary.

The Bristol building also employed the latest American practice in its use of an internal lift for the movement of goods. The first passenger lift had been installed in New York's Haughwout Building of 1857, and Richard Waygood introduced the first hydraulic passenger lifts to Britain in 1870. The use of lifts in the Granary dispensed with the need for external hoists that had been so conspicuous on earlier warehouses (including the Albert Dock), and further enabled the warehouse to be regarded as a piece of urban architecture, following the accepted canons of the time.

Templeton's Carpet Factory, Glasgow: W. Leiper, 1889.

A small part of the doorway to a school in Reading, built in 1885. In this section alone there are six different patterns of brick.

Fletton bricks
See North Harrow Estate, 1925
Gothic
See All Saints, Margaret St, 1855 and Manchester Town Hall, 1868
Palazzo
See Hamilton Square, 1830

Back-to-Back Houses, Leeds 1875

In *The Good Companions* (1929), J. B. Priestley describes back-to-back houses as 'the product of an ingenious architectural scheme that crammed four dwelling houses into the space of two and enabled some past citizens to drive a carriage and pair and take their wives and daughters to the Paris Exhibition of 1867'.

The 'ingenious architectural scheme' of back-to-backs was that only one wall of the dwelling had doors and windows set in it; the other three walls were shared with the neighbours. Back-to-backs emerged at the end of the 18th century as a very cheap solution to housing working people and, as a result, very attractive to the developer. Not only did they take up very little land, but they were also economic in their use of materials. With three of the four walls being shared with the neighbours, the back-to-back was obviously cheaper than a conventional terraced house with two external walls at the front and rear.

For the occupants the advantages of the design were not so evident. The lack of ventilation was an infamous problem, allowing air to stagnate and diseases to breed. Yet in bleak northern cities, when a ventilation system was actually provided by the developer, the residents often blocked up the ventilation holes, preferring stagnation to the howling draughts.

The earliest back-to-back dwellings were two storeys high and roughly square in plan, and their width (or frontage) varied from about 3–4.5 m. There were a number of later variations: some were built to three storeys, and some were built as maisonettes over single-storey 'through' units, which ran from one external wall to the other.

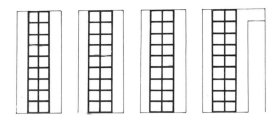

Development layout of typical back-to-backs (now demolished) in Commercial Road, Halifax. Each small square is a dwelling.

Density

One of the most important aspects of housing design is an understanding of the number of people who are going to live in a given unit of ground area. This figure is that of the 'density' of population and can be expressed as 'dwellings per hectare', 'bedspaces per hectare' or 'people per hectare'. The most common unit is people per hectare (ppha).

When construction of the infamous back-to-backs was at its peak, there were reports that suggested a level of 2000 ppha. In the 'great structure' of the **Boundary Street Estate, 1895**, 4600 people were rehoused in 4.5 hectares of land, giving an approximate density of 1000 ppha. The **Aylesbury Estate, 1977** was designed with a density of 326 ppha, so as we progress through the 20th century we can see a gradual reduction in the number of people expected to live in a given area of the inner city. Outside the inner city the density has always been lower. The Dudley Report, published in 1944, suggested a suburban density of up to 120 ppha, compared to double that density in the town centres.

Towards the end of the period in which back-to-backs were built in large quantities, the design had become virtually standard, with a cellar topped by two floors with two rooms each, and an attic above. Standardization of design was very important to the developer, as all of the components of the building, and its assembly, could be kept the same. Even at the edges of a back-to-back estate, where there was not enough room for a full two-fronted terrace, just one row of dwellings would be built and the central party wall left exposed. These were called 'half-backs' or 'salt-pie' houses, and many survive today. At the ends of the streets the design was often adapted so that the two end units became shops, with their display windows on the exposed side walls.

Back-to-backs were generally squalid and overcrowded. They were intended for the poorest members of society, and they were built neither to last, nor to look impressive. At the peak of their popularity they were built at a **density** of up to 350 dwellings per hectare, which probably represented some 2000 people per hectare.

As early as 1842 a Bill was introduced in the House of Lords which attempted to ban them, but the key clause in the Bill was dropped because some local authorities feared that the measure would force the cost of houses up so much that fewer affordable homes would be built as a consequence. Later in the 19th century, in response to growing criticism, a modification known as 'through-by-lights' was developed, where two dwellings interlocked, giving each a wide living room occupying one external wall, and a narrow scullery occupying the other, thus allowing a through draught of air. Back-to-backs were finally banned by Parliament in 1909. Those that survive are the best examples of the type, and not occupied by such large family units as in the 19th century. In 1980 it was made legal to construct them once again, but it is now required that back-to-back dwellings should have adequate cross-ventilation.

1 privy
2 yard
3 ashes
4 living room
5 up

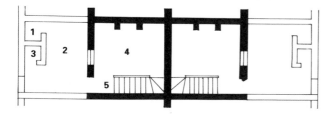

Ground-floor plan of two dwellings in Commercial Road, Halifax. Built in 1846, they were demolished in the mid-1960s. On the first floor there was one bedroom; another was in the attic.

Primrose Hill School, London 1885

The Queen Anne revival

Mark Girouard, who has written extensively on the subject, defined the so-called 'Queen Anne' style that prospered at the end of the 19th century as follows: '"Queen Anne" had relatively little to do with Queen Anne . . . It was the result of a group of the younger Gothicists becoming fed up with both the Gothic and the toughness of the 1860s. They thought up an ingenious new formula: Gothic bones, classical flesh. But the classicism which they favoured was . . . the vernacular classicism of Dutch canal-sides and 18th-century provincial towns.'

The resulting architecture resembled earlier Gothic buildings in that they were asymmetrical with a sharp, angular silhouette, but the detailed features were Dutch, with stepped gables and pretty wooden oriel windows. The leading practitioner in the Queen Anne style had been Norman Shaw, who was the most influential architect in late-19th-century Britain. Although the style was mainly associated with fashionable homes for the rich, it is interesting that poorer Londoners were eventually given access to it: first of all in the Board schools of the 1880s and then, a decade later, in the new homes that were being designed for them by the London County Council, of which the **Boundary Street Estate, 1895** is an excellent example.

In 1910 the Royal Institute of British Architects stated in its *Journal*: 'There is probably no type of modern building which more nearly combines the merits of carefully thought-out planning with an architectural treatment so thoroughly expressive of its purpose as a typical London Board school.'

The School Boards had been established by the Education Act of 1870 and survived until local authorities took over the responsibility for education in the early years of the next century. Until 1870 education had been provided by voluntary – especially religious – organizations, with only partial financial support from public sources. In the poorest areas so-called 'Ragged Schools' were built.

These early schools had been designed on the assumption that children would be taught in classes of over a hundred pupils, using the system of senior children acting as assistant teachers. The School Boards soon asserted their belief that class sizes should be smaller, with a teacher allocated to each, and the planning of the Board schools reflected this: instead of schools being just one huge open internal space (someone once said a barn would do), they became complex buildings divided into many smaller classrooms.

In the early days of the Boards, school halls were not provided, but it was soon realized that these provided a social focus for the school, as well being the hub of circulation, placed in the centre of the plan to reduce the number of corridors. Glazed partitions were provided between the classrooms, partly to allow the all-powerful head teacher to supervise what was going on in classrooms.

Most Board schools were erected in areas of high housing density and little available land. They thus had to be tall buildings. The characteristic 'three-decker' design evolved, creating three-storey schools standing like 'beacons' or 'ornaments' of the neighbourhood. Each with the capacity for well over a thousand children, their presence was supposed to act as a 'leavening influence' on the squalor around.

Birmingham's School Board built a number of new schools in the early 1890s, which, with their tall spires, were even more beacon-like. Designed by the local private architectural firm of Chamberlain & Martin, they were in a red-brick Gothic style, with much **terracotta** decoration. Examples survive in Bordesley and Small Heath.

The architectural style of schools was considered to be very important, and reflected the most progres-

White Star Offices, Liverpool: Norman Shaw, 1895.

Plough Road Board School, south London, 1890.

sive architectural thinking of the times. In London an orthodox, almost scholarly Gothic in the 1870s gave way to a more relaxed **Queen Anne** style in the 1880s, of which Primrose Hill School is an example. This was thought to express the 'civil rather than ecclesiastical character' of the buildings, and was also considered to be cheaper, offering the opportunity for more ornamentation, through simple brick modelling, than the Gothic style could. Architectural concerns affected even the most basic decisions about planning the new schools. although it was felt that the classrooms should face east to benefit from early sun, and the school hall should face west, it was also thought that the classrooms should ideally face away from the street towards the rear of the building, because their appearance was considered too uniform for a piece of urban architecture.

The Boards understood that an investment in architectural decoration was necessary. One Board architect noted that 'it was found that the difference of cost between bare utilitarianism and buildings designed in some sort of style . . . was rather less than 5 per cent' – exactly the same proportion of overall cost that was being invested in speculative housing at the same time. (See also the notes on brick manufacture in **The Granary, 1869**.)

In the capital the London County Council took over the Board's responsibility for education In 1903, and its architects continued the Board's tradition of providing buildings as a social service – a tradition that survived until the Inner London Education Authority was abolished in 1989.

1 **lavatory**
2 **hall**
3 **classroom**

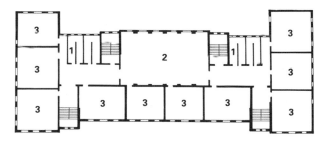

Plan of Fulham Palace Road Board School, London, 1902.

Schools
See also Templewood School, 1949 and Burnham Copse School, 1986
Terracotta
See Manchester Town Hall, 1868

145 Buccleuch Street, Glasgow 1892

Glasgow has a reputation for a unique tradition of **tenement housing**. In truth thousands of people have lived, and still do live, in tenements in every large British city; what is unique about Glasgow is that tenement living was also experienced by the middle-class population, for whom many private blocks were constructed in the years leading up to the First World War.

Until the middle of the 19th century the Glasgow tenements were almost exclusively occupied by the labouring classes, but thereafter more prosperous people began to live in them without stigma. This enabled the city to achieve a uniformity of architectural character, while allowing both social and architectural diversity to flourish within it.

The tenement block was usually three or four storeys high, with either two or three flats grouped around the staircase, depending on the status of the building. In Glasgow parlance the flats were known as 'houses', and the stair as the 'close'.

The plan of a typical tenement shows how three houses are grouped tightly around the common stair. Entry to the stair would be directly off the street and, uniquely to Glasgow, the Corporation would often be responsible for the lighting of the stair. Two of the houses would run the full depth of the building, each with two principal rooms. All the occupants would sleep in bed recesses, which would each contain a double bed and be screened off from the rest of the room.

A third, much smaller dwelling would be at the back of the building. Sometimes this would only have one room: when it did, it was known as a 'single-end'. All three dwellings would share the lavatory on the landing off the stair.

The problem with so many of the Glasgow tenements was rarely to do with the quality of the building itself, but with overcrowding. Frequently a single-end would be occupied by more than one family. Legislation was passed to prevent overcrowding, and consequently most of the buildings in the poorer areas no longer survive.

By comparison, No. 145 Buccleuch Street was in a well-to-do district and represented a much more genteel lifestyle. It is a very late example of the tenement type – much of the area around it in Garnethill had already been developed by the middle of the century. The undeveloped site was acquired by a local builder in 1892, and plans were drawn up for a four-storey development of seven 'closes', comprising 56 dwellings in all.

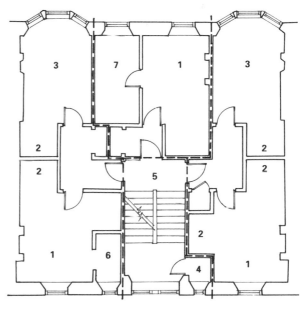

Plan of a typical Glasgow tenement, of a humbler type than that at Buccleuch Street.

1 **living/kitchen**
2 **bed**
3 **sitting**
4 **lavatory**
5 **stair**
6 **scullery**
7 **bedroom**

Access in housing blocks

The design of the large, multi-storey tenement housing block requires careful consideration of the way in which people move from the public street at ground level, to the front doors of their dwellings.

Before the development of lifts the only form of access was by stair, and this limited the height of blocks to four or five storeys at the very maximum (nowadays three storeys are considered the maximum for people to climb). Two arrangements were used, one being the 'walk-up' or 'direct' form of access. This requires a large number of staircases, because every flat is entered directly off a staircase landing, with two, or maybe four flats per landing.

Glasgow tenements all adopted the walk-up principle. So too did the **Boundary Street Estate, 1895**, where there had been much debate during its design about whether it was economical to provide two front doors per landing.

Not only was the walk-up system costly due to the number of staircases needed, but it often led to the creation of dark and dingy landings, in which the front doors were placed very near to the centre of the building.

The other approach, which was much cheaper to construct, was the 'gallery', 'deck' or 'balcony' system, in which just one staircase led to an open balcony at each level, which then led to each front

door. It is easy to see how this system made dwelling blocks look like barracks. Later on, in the 1980s, the system was vigorously criticized for not allowing residents any 'defensible space' (or space they could call their own) outside their front doors, and **Alice Coleman** blamed it for much of the social breakdown prevalent on housing estates. In the period following the Second World War further developments experimented with internal corridors, which gave access to front doors on either side and were permanently artificially lit (see p. 113, illustrations). There were also 'point blocks', in which one 'point' of circulation with lifts was placed right in the centre of the building, and as large a number of flats as possible were accessed from it. **Alpha House, 1962** employed this system, with six flats per storey grouped around the central lift shaft.

Alice Coleman
See Aylesbury Estate, 1977
Deck access
See p. 112, illustration, in Alton West Estate, 1959
Queen Anne
See Primrose Hill School, 1885
Tenement housing
See also Boundary Street Estate, 1895; Alton West Estate, 1959; Alpha House, 1962; Aylesbury Estate, 1977; Mercers House, 1992

As with much speculative housebuilding, finances for Buccleuch Street were very tight. Original proposals for a more flamboyant architectural style in something like the **Queen Anne** idiom were abandoned on grounds of cost, and building proceeded with a much barer treatment of the façade. Then, after the first of the dwellings had been completed (No. 145 was one of them), the builder had to sell them off immediately to fund the remaining development.

No. 145 is of particular interest. Currently owned by the National Trust for Scotland, it was formerly occupied by a Miss Toward from 1911–65, and the interior is virtually as she left it. Her life has been recorded in a Trust publication entitled *Miss Toward of the Tenement House*. This recounts how she worked as a shorthand typist, and enjoyed the theatre and music. In addition, she was a regular member of the Woman's Guild, and the local kirk, and she always voted Conservative at election time.

But Miss Toward's comfortable lifestyle was far from that of the typical tenement dweller, and the unromantic squalor of Glasgow's overcrowded tenements has long been superseded by redevelopment.

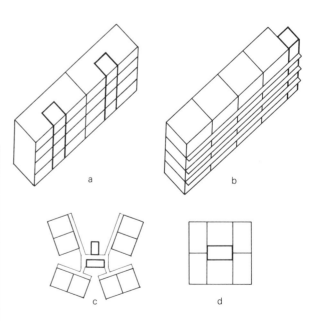

Types of access: (a) walk-up flats; (b) deck-access flats; (c) a 'cluster block' with eight maisonettes on each storey, 1955 – this is Keeling House in Bethnal Green, designed by Denys Lasdun, and 'listed' by the government in 1993; (d) Alpha House – a point block.

Boundary Street Estate, London 1895

Boundary Street Estate, London 1895

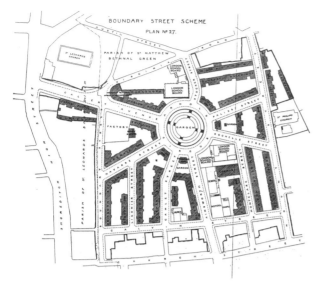

Plan of the new estate at Boundary Street.

The bandstand, Boundary Street.

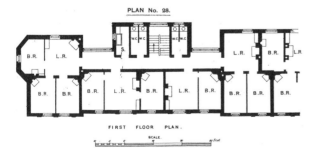

Plan of one of the blocks at Boundary Street, showing four dwellings grouped around a stair, with communal WCs and scullery.

Chertsey House.

What was new at Boundary Street was that even the poorest members of society were entitled to live in what could be termed 'architecture', instead of in barracks like Verandah Cottages (see p. 27, top illustration).

After the **London County Council** (LCC) was formed in 1889, it took advantage of new legislation that enabled it to remove old slum areas and replace them with new housing. The laws required that these developments should be designed to house exactly the same number of people as had been displaced, which meant that they had to be of a high **density**. Since it was also important to provide as much open space as possible at ground level, the new buildings had to be tall, rising to five or six storeys.

The LCC's first great development was at Boundary Street in London's Bethnal Green. This estate replaced the infamous Old Nichol slums, which were a warren of courts and alleys and had one of the greatest crime rates in 19th-century London. Infant mortality ran at one child in four, and it was written of the area that 'in subterranean basements men and women have swarmed and bred and died like wolves in their lairs'. The clearance of the slums was made under the Housing of the Working Classes Act of 1890, and was completed by 1895. The LCC instructed its newly formed architects' department to prepare designs for the estate, which it undertook in a strong spirit of social purpose and creativity.

An estimated 5719 people had lived in the Old Nichol area, and the target for the new scheme was to rehouse 4600 (the difference being taken up in a small adjacent estate).

The architects swept away the last vestiges of the old street pattern, and replaced it with a system of wide roads radiating from a central open space, which was formed on raised ground, using the soil dug for the new buildings' foundations. On this they placed a bandstand – a demonstration of the LCC's self appointed mission not only to provide for peoples' housing needs, but to add to their quality of life as well. The architect in charge of the scheme imagined courting couples strolling around the bandstand on summer evenings (a thought that would not have entered Scott's mind when he laid out Akroydon 30 years earlier).

A variety of blocks were designed to suit different sizes of household, although the LCC had a policy not to provide accommodation for single people. All the blocks were arranged to form courtyards within which there was provision for refuse collection and storage for costermongers' barrows. Access to the front doors was from the main street, and there was usually a flourish of decoration around the doorways. Communal laundries, shops and meeting rooms were also provided, so that the new estate became a self-contained community.

Although the entire scheme was built at the same time, there is great variety in the architectural treatment of the blocks. These were early days for the LCC architects: later a 'house style' would emerge, causing much of inner London to be covered with identical blocks of tenements. The dominant style of the Boundary Street decoration followed the most progressive ideas of the end of the 19th century. It reflects the influence of Norman Shaw and the Queen Anne revival (which at Boundary Street was most evident in the earlier blocks around the bandstand), and the **arts and crafts** movement. Many influential architects of that movement, such as Philip Webb, W. R. Lethaby and William Morris, all had close associations with the new housing branch of the LCC, to the extent that one of the Boundary Street Estate's architects even stated: 'Anything I know about architecture is due to Philip Webb.'

Immediately after the construction of Boundary Street, the LCC went on to build the Millbank Estate on the site of an old penitentiary. Started in 1899, it is architecturally much more consistent than Boundary Street. It housed 4430 people in 896 dwellings, and was a perfectly symmetrical composition around a central garden. Susan Beattie, in her book *A Revolution in London Housing* (1980), wrote of Millbank that 'its elegance remains undiminished today, a stirring memorial . . . to Victorian social conscience and to the committed endeavour of local government to improve the quality of Londoners' lives'.

The arts and crafts movement
This was initiated by an informal grouping of designers – influenced by William Morris, W. R. Lethaby, Norman Shaw and Philip Webb – active in the 1880s and 90s. In many ways running parallel to similar developments in Continental Europe, the arts and crafts movement was sensitive to the way in which things were made, and in particular the materials they were made from. Romantically inspired by the Middle Ages, which it believed was dominated by craft production, it stood against the increasing industrialization of artefacts. But it was ultimately only of appeal to the rich, who could afford to commission its bespoke craft items. From the 1930s onwards the movement rose in historical importance due to the writings of Nikolaus Pevsner, who saw it as one of the key constituents of the Modern movement in architecture, which he so vigorously promoted.

An internal courtyard, Millbank Estate, 1899.

Density	Tenement housing
See Back-to-Back Houses, 1875	See also 145 Buccleuch Street, 1892;
London County Council	Alton West Estate, 1959;
See also Primrose Hill School, 1885; Royal Festival Hall, 1951; Alton West Estate, 1959	Alpha House, 1962; Aylesbury Estate, 1977; Mercers House, 1992

The Boston, London 1899

The mid-1890s was a boom time for pub building, and the Boston's prestigious position on a prominent road and omnibus route intersection in Tufnell Park, London, makes it one of the best of the time. So does its architectural treatment, in which there was a considerable investment by the original landlord to make a building that was attractive enough to entice passers-by to enter.

By the 1890s social drinking had changed dramatically since the days of the gin palace in the 1830s, with its reputation for debauchery and child drunkenness. Slum clearance had done away with many of the small old drinking houses, and magistrates and local authorities were reluctant to license new premises.

Even if the large new establishments like the Boston were more sophisticated, they still catered for a very specific section of the population – the working man and, not infrequently, woman. But in the late 19th century, pubs were much more of a centre of social life than they are today. They were used for auctions and sporting events, and even as employment exchanges. Closed societies would use them for their meetings, for there were usually private rooms to hire. Landlords would even let customers roast their Sunday joints in the pub oven for a small fee.

The late-19th-century pub is the best surviving statement in architecture of the aesthetic and social aspirations of the majority of the population. The churches did not need to advertise themselves, and housebuilders frequently did not have the resources for this. The pub alone survives in sufficient numbers to tell us what the Victorian working class considered to be tasteful (and what, of course, the classes above considered to be vulgar). Generally the architects who designed pubs were specialists in this field and, though frequently prosperous, were looked down upon by the rest of their profession. They were above all else experts in applying the huge number of ready-made mass-produced ornaments on to a pub's façade.

The architects of the Boston were a firm called Thorpe & Furniss, who were very successful in this field at the time. They were quite happy working in any style, or derivative of style, according to the budget and the tastes of the landlord. Clearly a pub occupying such a prominent position as the Boston's needed to be conspicuous from a distance. To help achieve this, it was given a massive round tower embellished with clocks and rising five storeys above the pavement. The external architectural decoration is equally lavish, with pilasters surrounding the tower

The details of the façade of the Boston are in Portland stone rather than cheaper stucco.

and modelling around all the windows. Everything is in Portland stone, not stucco, and no expense has been spared, even down to the specially carved plaque above the entrance.

The fantasy architecture of pubs was particularly important at the entrance, which was frequently lined with decorative tiles and brightly lit. Even though electricity was commonly available for lighting at the end of the century, on a dark evening the pub would have been the brightest thing in the street. The interiors too were full of decorative lamps, with sumptuous carving and metalwork, but sadly the Boston's original interior no longer survives.

Stylistically the Boston is a mixture of a number of themes that had been established by 'élite' architecture some ten or more years before. There are elements of the **Queen Anne revival**, happily intermixed with the **classical orders**. It may be a very unscholarly piece of architecture, but it is lively in the extreme. It is easy to criticize pub architecture as being vulgar, but if we do that, we are really only admitting that pubs served a social function that we consider beneath us. If architecture is the business of making buildings communicate messages, then the 19th-century pub was just as valid architecturally as the great churches and country houses.

Classical orders
See Bank of England, 1844
Queen Anne revival
See Primrose Hill School, 1885

51–57 Ivydale Road, London 1900

Life in one of the 19th-century London **suburbs** has been described beautifully in George and Weedon Grossmith's *Diary of a Nobody* (1892). The suburbs had started to grow from the 1860s, when organized systems of public transport could take the suburban dwellers to their urban places of work, and these new developments accounted for the largest growth in population throughout the whole country between 1881 and 1891.

Ivydale Road in south London is one such suburb. It was part of the Waverley Park Estate in Nunhead, which was developed by Edward Yates from 1884 onwards. Of some 20 hectares, the estate took 20 years to complete, financed by a complex system of loans. These were boom years for speculative housing in the inner suburbs of the major cities.

Yates built for the respectable end of the market, and he invested in quality in the design and construction of his houses in order to convey the social standing of their inhabitants. The external appearance of houses of this period offers a profound insight into social values; their design being much more about displaying status than simply 'taste' alone.

The façades of terraced houses had gradually evolved from the uniformity of the Palladian model, which survived up to the middle of the century (see **Hamilton Square, 1830**), into styles expressing much greater individuality. By contrast to the Palladian terrace, which tried to make the whole block look like one building, perhaps with a central emphasis, and disguising the appearance of front doors, the late-19th-century house attempted to make each dwelling look like a building on its own, rather than just part of a terrace. One reason for this increase in the emphasis on the individual dwelling was the rise in home ownership, financed through building society loans, as opposed to the leasehold and rental system that had been common earlier.

A number of motifs were used to create the illusion of individuality. The most important was the bay window, which had become virtually obligatory by the end of the century. On 'lower-class' houses the bay might be in the ground floor only, but as the status of the house increased, so would the importance of the bay: perhaps it would be surmounted by a make-believe balcony; perhaps it would occupy the full height of the building; and perhaps it might be crowned by its own small gable, reminiscent of a stately Tudor house.

The frontage of the speculative house evolved into a very sophisticated series of 'thresholds' controlling the transition from the public world of the street to the private world of the interior. On more substantial homes there would be a small front 'garden' surrounded by a hedge or railings, and a gate: the first threshold to be crossed. Then a step, a porch and a

1 **scullery**
2 **kitchen/living**
3 **living room**
4 **front room**

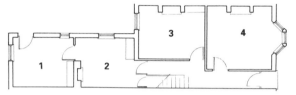

Plan of one of the houses in Ivydale Road. This plan was a standard type for houses of this size all over the country.

The way in which the same house can be given different social status by architectural additions: (a) plain, flat façade; (b) bay window to ground floor only; (c) bay window to both floors; (d) the full works: bay windows, little gable, front garden with hedge.

front door had to be crossed or passed through. Even though these thresholds took up the minimum of space, they were very potent symbols of property and privacy. This is the 'defensible space' that was thought to be so lacking in many of the housing schemes of the 20th century (see **Aylesbury Estate, 1977**). Views of the interior were similarly controlled. In the bay window, curtains, net curtains, and pot plants would be used to prevent privacy being compromised.

The façade of the speculative house of the turn of the century would be adorned with expensive **bricks**, in contrast to the ordinary bricks used for the rear and internal walls. The bricks that were in fashion at any time were the ones that cost more, and this cost reflected the techniques of manufacture and distribution that were current then. Yates had established his own brickfields on the site of his new buildings, but he would also have had to import building materials by rail; indeed, he even set up his own siding for deliveries by train.

No professional architects were used in the design of these buildings, but developers like Yates were helped by a journal called the *Illustrated Carpenter and Builder*, in which designs were suggested. Articles went into great detail about the specification of materials, as well as prices. One article describes a house 'for £100' in Liverpool and details the special red **bricks** that were to be used on the façade, and their cost. They were to come from Ruabon in north Wales and cost some £4 and 10 shillings (£4.50) – or 4.5 per cent of the total cost – more than ordinary bricks. Such was the importance of decoration (see also **Primrose Hill School, 1885**).

At a cost of £190 each, the houses at Nos. 51–57 Ivydale Road were much more substantial than the Liverpool dwellings of £100 each, and they had more embellishments. There were mouldings around the front door and the bay window, and a small front garden – all designed to convey the feeling of dignity desired by the potential occupants. Even the street names continued the theme: Ivydale, Rosenthorpe, Limesford and Hawkeslade – they all connoted romantic detachment from the reality of the suburb they were actually in.

Architectural ornamentation around one of the windows in Ivydale Road.

Bricks
See topic under The Granary, 1869
Suburbs
See Rushby Mead, 1911; North Harrow Estate, 1925; Jaywick Sands, 1930; Chelmer Village, 1974

Lion Chambers, Glasgow 1905

This eight-storey office block in the centre of Glasgow is one of the pioneers of the use of **reinforced concrete** construction in Britain. Despite this, its appearance remains conventional, owing much to the Scottish tradition of decoration of commercial buildings. In the latter part of the 19th century, Glasgow, like Liverpool and Manchester, had been energetically reinterpreting the architecture of the Italian **palazzo** and the established **Gothic** precedent for its new commercial premises. But Glasgow had also been closely watching the latest developments on Continental Europe, as well as maintaining a reverence for its own particularly Scottish traditions of architecture.

The designers of Lion Chambers were James Salmon, junior, and J. G. Gillespie. Salmon was a friend of Charles Rennie Mackintosh, one of the most influential pioneers of the **Modern movement** in architecture, who had founded the world-famous Glasgow School of Art less than ten years before. Salmon had also been the architect of one of the city's most exuberant early office buildings – the so-called 'Hatrack' of 1899, which has been claimed to be closer to Continental art nouveau than have any works of the better-known Mackintosh. Another eight-storey building, the Hatrack is almost as lively in design as buildings by such European contemporaries as the Belgian Victor Horta, the Frenchman Hector Guimard or the highly individual Catalan Antonio Gaudí.

But Lion Chambers is altogether different in concept. There may be a number of traditional features – a typically Glaswegian corner turret; a pair of steep gables on the roof, facing south and west; a careful modelling of the external wall surface and gathering of the windows into simple but convincing patterns – but for all this the walls are bare, white concrete.

Lion Chambers uses the French Hennebique system of construction. Systems for building with reinforced concrete were developed in both the USA and France from the 1870s onwards, and they offered an alternative to the steel frame (which is not so fireproof) as a way of building tall buildings with large, open floor areas.

Like the steel frame, reinforced concrete also allows very large window openings to be inserted. Although Lion Chambers' most conspicuous façades are traditional in design, with small windows, the north wall is almost completely glazed, allowing a large amount of light into the offices. The architecture of this wall makes an interesting comparison with that of **Oriel Chambers, 1864** in Liverpool and with early

Reinforced concrete

Concrete is made by mixing cement with aggregates, such as sand and small stones, and water. When poured into a mould and allowed to set, it acquires the strength of stone. And, like stone, it is strong when it is in compression. In other words, it can cope with the pressure of much weight on it. But like stone too, it is not strong in tension. Tension occurs when a simple beam is required to span a long distance. The force of gravity causes the beam to bend (or 'deflect') downwards, and as a result its lower surface is stretched so that, if the beam is made from stone or concrete, it breaks.

In the early 19th century, builders had begun to make concrete floors by filling concrete between iron girders. But it was not until the end of the century that a truly scientific understanding was developed of the process of placing steel bars within the concrete while it is being moulded. In this way the resulting reinforced concrete will be strong in tension, as well as compression, and will also be completely fireproof. Much of the work of today's structural engineers is in designing the exact diameter and positioning of these bars.

cast-iron buildings in Glasgow. It reached its ultimate form of expression in the development of the **curtain wall**.

The Hennebique system used square concrete posts to support horizontal beams. On these beams sat flat floor slabs, all of which had stout reinforcing bars embedded within them to ensure that the material was strong in tension as well as compression.

It was very unusual for reinforced concrete to be used for the external walls of buildings, as well as the structural frame. Throughout the 20th century, up to the present day, the external walls of concrete-framed buildings have usually been clad in different materials, whether modern in manufacture and concept, or traditional. But at Lion Chambers, *in situ* concrete was used throughout, allowing the external walls to be very thin. In this context, *in situ* means 'cast in its place', indicating that the walls are made from concrete that has been moulded in its final position, instead of from bricks or blocks. This allows thinner walls to be constructed: at only 100 mm in thickness, the walls of Lion Chambers enabled the internal space to be of a practical size. Thicker walls would have eaten away too much of this internal space.

St Jean de Montmartre, Paris: Anatole de Baudot, 1894. The first church to be built with a reinforced-concrete skeleton and enclosed by thin external walls.

The use of *in situ* concrete construction for an
entire building, including its external walls, may seem
a simple idea, but it has never been very popular. As a
material, concrete is difficult to mould: the timber
'formwork' may often be as complex in construction
as a timber building in its own right, and when the
structure is finished, the formwork is simply dis-
carded. In addition, **brutalist** concrete buildings can be
seen to weather badly, particularly in the British climate. And walls of such slenderness as those of Lion
Chambers have nothing near the requisite qualities of
heat insulation that today's standards demand.
Despite these negative attributes, the reinforced-
concrete internal frame, with its large internal spaces,
and totally fireproof qualities, became the century's
most striking structural innovation in the design of
urban buildings.

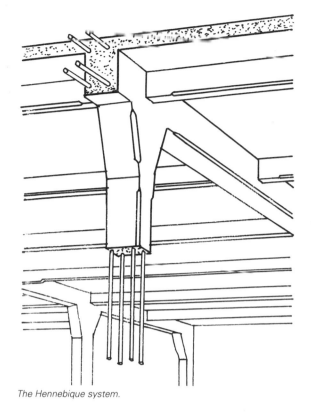

The Hennebique system.

The north wall of Lion Chambers.

Brutalism
See Crown Offices, 1980
Curtain wall
See Peter Jones, 1935 and
Willis, Faber & Dumas, 1975
Gothic
See All Saints, Margaret St,
1855
Modern movement
See Wicklands Avenue, 1934
Office buildings
See Bank of England, 1844;
Oriel Chambers, 1864; Lion
Chambers, 1905; Willis Faber &
Dumas, 1975; Hillingdon Civic
Centre, 1977; Crown Offices,
1980; Canary Wharf, 1990
Palazzo
See Hamilton Square, 1830

Selfridges, London 1907

Selfridges store in Oxford Street, London, marks the coming together of two great architectural traditions in one building: one is the **classical** tradition – and the exterior of Selfridges is as strong a classical composition as you will see anywhere; the other is the newer tradition of building using a steel frame. In other words, Selfridges combines a new construction technique with a very traditional form of external decoration.

The building shows us just how much effort a commercial developer is prepared to put into creating architectural ornament, for which – of course – there must be a purpose. With a sense of paternalism that was typical of the time, Gordon Selfridge stated how 'it was the duty of the great business house to unite beauty with its effort'. A less pious thought would have been to admit that 'beauty' demonstrated through architecture is good business.

Let us look at that massive and confident façade that towers over Oxford Street. It took over 20 years to complete, for the site was previously a jumble of Georgian-type buildings that had slowly come into Selfridges' ownership. It is therefore remarkable that the design that was established for the first (most easterly) phase was continued seamlessly westwards until the store's completion in 1928.

Detail of the façade of Selfridges.

Edwardian Grand Manner

We have noted how the architectural historian Nikolaus Pevsner once described the 19th century as the 'Fancy Dress Ball of Architecture' (see **Manchester Town Hall, 1868**). From the middle of the century onwards architects argued passionately in favour of one style or another, be it Venetian Gothic or Palladian. For a time classical architecture was decidedly out of fashion – even the great classical Roman textbook by Vitruvius was declared in the *Architect* of 1883 to be so much 'waste paper'. But 20 years later classicism was back in vogue, championed by large public buildings like the War Office in Whitehall of 1899 and Belfast City Hall of 1897.

The same architect of Belfast City Hall, Sir A. Brumwell Thomas, also built Stockport Town Hall in 1904 (see bottom illustration on p. 32), basing his design on the English classicists Wren and Hawksmoor. The influences on what came to be called the Grand Manner were not just this English Baroque, but also the French École des Beaux-Arts, where a number of influential British architects of the period had studied. But this most pompous period in British architecture had dwindled away by the outset of the First World War. The Fancy Dress Ball was over, at least for the time being.

King Edward VII Galleries, British Museum, London: John Burnet,
1904.

That initial design had been established by Francis Swales, a young American architect who had studied in Paris at the highly influential École des Beaux-Arts. This school had been founded by Napoleon in 1806, and strongly reasserted the role of architecture as a fine art within the classical tradition. Swales's design for Selfridges had followed another even more strongly Beaux-Arts-influenced scheme in London: this was the new extension to the British Museum that had been started in 1904 by John Burnet, a celebrated Glasgow architect who had also studied in Paris. The British Museum extension is ponderously classical with an array of Ionic columns along its vast façade.

The Selfridges façade also features a giant Ionic

colonnade, but it is handled in a completely different way. Between the museum's columns are conventional classical windows, detailed in a way that has clearly come from the **palazzo** tradition. But Selfridges introduced into Britain an architectural device that allowed for much larger areas of glass within the classical framework. If you look at the illustration on p. 63 and blur your eyes, you can see it: in between the huge Ionic columns everything is dark. Each floor is glazed with large windows, and at the points where the floors themselves meet the façade there are dark metal 'spandrel' panels. It is as if the modern steel box (which is what Selfridges really is) is trying to squeeze out from behind the colonnade.

The style is very American: indeed, while the British Museum is, through Burnet, British/French in design, Selfridges is American/French. Swales's collaborator on the design was the well-known Chicago architect Daniel Burnham, who had been responsible for many of the tallest buildings in that city during its rapid expansion over the previous two decades. The so-called Chicago school of architecture had, through the 1890s, dispensed with all the superfluous stonework on a building's façade, and allowed the skyscrapers' internal steel frames to dictate what was seen on the exterior. Huge steel-framed towers of up to 16 storeys high were crammed into the city's streets, and they gradually abandoned the old rules of classical composition.

But Selfridges was no skyscraper, and it kept its classical colonnade. The architect in charge of its later phases was the same (now Sir) John Burnet of the British Museum. He had, in the meantime, given London one of its first truly American-style office blocks in Kodak House in Kingsway. This also had a steel frame, but none of the exuberant classical detailing of Selfridges.

The Beaux-Arts tradition in Britain disappeared with the outbreak of the First World War. Historians believed that they could see an altogether new type of architecture emerging, without all that classical detailing. Many architects of the mid-20th century looked back at Selfridges as if it was almost prehistoric in design, just because Gordon Selfridge wanted to advertise his business with a confident display of classicism in stone. But lurking beneath the classicism, the building was actually thoroughly modern and thoroughly American.

Kodak House, Kingsway, London: John Burnet, 1910.

Rushby Mead, Letchworth 1911

Established in 1903, Letchworth was the first garden city – the forerunner of Welwyn Garden City and all the British **new towns**. Although it is a commuter town today, the intention of Letchworth's founders was that it should be one of a number of garden cities, joined to each other in a framework of towns, countryside and interconnecting communications that tried to find a happy balance between the city, with its overcrowding, squalor and high land value, and the countryside with its open space.

The theoretical framework for the garden cities was devised by Ebenezer Howard. Born in 1850, he was commited to social reform. He had spent his mid-twenties in the USA, and soon after his return he became a shorthand writer to the Royal Commission on labour, gaining first-hand experience of the social reform movement of the time. He had also become well acquainted with the earliest attempts to provide model colonies for workers, from New Lanark, founded in 1780, to Cadbury's Bournville of 1895 (see **Akroydon, 1861**).

Howard was also an inventor, and he spent much of his life trying to develop a shorthand typewriter. He was fascinated with systems, and this led him to create the garden city idea. His book, *Tomorrow: A Peaceful Path to Real Reform*, was published in 1898 and republished in 1902 under its more familiar title, *Garden Cities of Tomorrow*. It contains many now famous diagrams, which are so obviously the work of an inventor of machines. They show theoretical 'Garden Cities' of about 32 000 people grouped around a 'Central City' of 58 000 people. The inter-municipal railways and roads follow logical paths. Each individual garden city was to be based on a grid of radiating and concentric roads, with a 'garden' at the very centre.

The key to the concept was the relationship between the town and the country, which was not just to do with access to open space, but also concerned the fact that industrial and agricultural economies would benefit mutually from such a relationship, owing to clearly formulated strategies for funding and the distribution of dividends for the common good. Garden cities were intended to be economically self-sufficient.

Although the first appearance of his book attracted

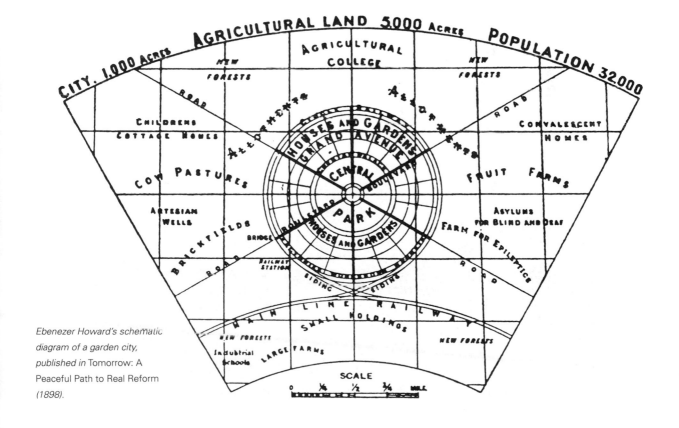

Ebenezer Howard's schematic diagram of a garden city, published in Tomorrow: A Peaceful Path to Real Reform (1898).

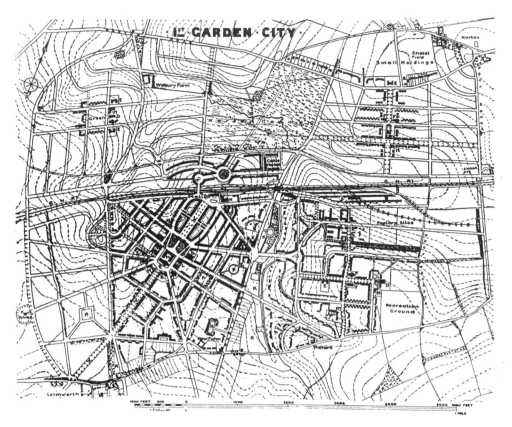

Plan of the first garden city.

The architecture of the early houses in Letchworth owed much to the vernacular style of Kent and Sussex.

a great deal of scorn – 'as useful as would be the arrangements for protection against visits from Mr Wells's Martians' were the words of the *Fabian News* – Howard had also attracted some powerful supporters.

In 1899 the Garden City Association was formed, and promoted a series of conferences. Three years later a company was established with the aim of finding and buying the land for the first garden city. Sites in Staffordshire, Warwickshire and Sussex were considered, but eventually an estate in Hertfordshire that included the village of Letchworth – then only with 450 inhabitants – was chosen. Howard's supporters were in a position to purchase nearly 1600 hectares of land and put those theoretical diagrams into practice.

In 1904 it was decided to proceed with a plan designed by a young north country pair of Barry Parker and Raymond Unwin. The original plan, which is preserved in Letchworth, is a clear adaptation of Howard's diagrammatic plans to suit the particular site. The 1906 guidebook to Letchworth decribed the situation as it was then.

'For the Central Square of the town a level plateau has been chosen near the existing station. It is marked on the spot by three isolated oak trees . . . the roads radiating from this Central Square, which will give ready access to all parts of the town, have been so planned that glimpses of the open countryside will be obtainable along them from the heart of the town, while they will afford to those approaching from the outskirts good views of the central buildings.'

The new housing got under way as soon as the garden city was established. The earliest homes were substantial detached houses, and among them is 'Arunside', which originally belonged to Parker and Unwin, who were responsible for the design of many of the early buildings and estates in Letchworth, including Rushby Mead, which has recently been refurbished in the colours of early Letchworth – off-white rough render with rich green doors and downpipes. Happily, all of these features are legally preserved by covenant, and although Letchworth has now moved far from the pioneering days of the 'First Garden City', the confidence of its early architecture, so powerfully suggesting a rural **suburbia**, is still there for us to see.

New towns
See Milton Keynes Central, 1979
Suburbia
See 51–57 Ivydale Road, 1900; North Harrow Estate, 1925; Jaywick Sands, 1930; Chelmer Village, 1974
Vernacular architecture
See Chelmer Village, 1974

North Harrow Estate, London 1925

Following the great 19th-century development of suburbs, the next energetic phase of expansion was in the period between the two world wars, in which four million new homes were built. Once again, these took advantage of new transport links.

The Metropolitan railway promoted the construction of new estates around its recently electrified lines in north-west London, under the romantic name of 'Metroland'. Other new estates catered for the motor car, which was soon to come within the buying power of lower-middle-class families.

Some of these new suburbs were municipal, while others were privately built by speculators with the principal aim of making a profit. The attractions to the developer were immense. Under the Housing Act of 1919 the government was prepared to hand out £160 for each house with a total floor area of under 85 square metres – which amounted to a quarter of its selling price of, say, £750. People whose annual income was about £250, and who could afford the mortgage, were desperate to escape into the 'tonic air' of the new suburbs. And, if they could not afford the mortgage, there was always the option of renting from the developer. An advert for the North Harrow Estate claimed 'Repayment as Rent arranged – Hundreds have been satisfied'.

In order for the developers to obtain maximum profits, it was vital that speculative suburbia was built as cheaply as possible, and yet appeared to the new occupants to have all the trappings of gentility. The principal feature of suburban design was the semi-detached dwelling. The Bedford Park Suburb to the west of London, which was begun in 1875, had established a new design model for suburbia and had asserted the semi-detached type in preference to the old terrace. The design of the 'semi-d' had many advantages: for the builder the shared party wall between the dwellings represented a valuable saving when compared to a detached house. (We have already seen how this particular economy was taken to extremes with the **back-to-back** format, which had three party walls.) For the consumer the semi-detached design gave easy access to the rear garden and coalshed, and allowed for a garage, which was often an optional extra. But, most of all, it contrasted with the loathed terraced housing that people were leaving.

The entrances to semi-detached homes were usually in opposite corners, giving the illusion that each of the pair was a completely separate building.

Bedford Park suburb: Richard Norman Shaw, 1875.

The ubiquitous building type (constructed in 1927 in the Wirral), this semi-detached house is almost identical to those in Harrow. The arched porch, the lack of a front gable, and the gabled side wall are all only cosmetic differences.

Fletton bricks

The clay from which the coarse pink Fletton bricks are made extends from Peterborough to Milton Keynes. There are carbon deposits within the clay, which means that it can burn by itself. The unpopularity of Fletton bricks led, by the 1930s, to sandfaced and rustic versions coming on to the market. For further notes on brick manufacture see **The Granary, 1869**.

Back-to-Backs
See Back-to-Back houses, 1875
Suburbia
See 51–57 Ivydale Road, 1900; Rushby Mead, 1911; Jaywick Sands, 1930; Chelmer Village, 1974

The dwellings were set back within a small ornamental front garden screened from the road. The front living room and bedroom above it had bay windows, which had become an almost compulsory indicator of social standing. Further embellishments were coloured leaded glass in the windows and small gables with painted timber nailed to them to look like traditional Tudor architecture.

Despite all these features that suggested individuality, suburbia as a whole was a place of ruthless monotony. The developers had no interest in providing real variation in their designs, which were built as far as possible out of standard components. Timber windows were mass-produced and often imported from abroad, and the cheapest bricks were used for the walls. On the front of the house these **fletton bricks** would be disguised by a coat of pebbledash. The formula was repeated without interruption throughout entire estates, or, as Arthur Edwards wrote in *The Design of Suburbia* (1981), like 'a scratched gramophone record which repeats interminably the same fragment of tune'.

Suburbia was built for a single class of occupant, and with a single type of building. With a **density** of 20 to 36 dwellings per hectare, it was too spread out to have a coherent form. In places like Bexley, or Sidcup, or North Harrow, **suburbia** just went on and on without interruption.

People, from architectural writers to pop groups, have loved to mock suburbia, and yet its buildings represent the most enduring and ubiquitous type of architecture in contemporary Britain.

1 kitchen
2 dining room
3 drawing room
4 bedroom
5 bathroom

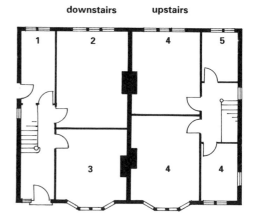

Typical design of a semi-detached house. Front elevation above, with plans of ground floor (left) and first floor (right).

Ibrox Stadium, Glasgow 1928

The street façade of the main stand showing Leitch's 'architectural'
public face of ornamental red brick.

The magnificent main stand at Rangers FC's Ibrox Stadium in Glasgow has survived intensive rebuilding of the ground in the 1980s, and was itself transformed in 1991, when an additional upper tier of 7300 seats was provided on top of the existing stand.

The structure had been built in 1928 after the club had won both the Scottish League and Cup. It was designed by Archibald Leitch, a Scottish engineer and architect who had trained in maritime engineering but came to specialize in football ground design, and achieved a high reputation within this specialism, designing major stands at clubs including Everton, Blackburn Rovers, Chelsea, Fulham, Sheffield Wednesday, Arsenal, Sunderland and Portsmouth. Examples at Everton, Sunderland and Portsmouth, as well as Ibrox, still survive.

If Leitch's work was not structurally adventurous, it is certainly memorable, and was, until the advent of the cantilever stands of the 1950s onwards, the 'state of the art' in British stadium design. The Ibrox stand was perhaps the most majestic, but certainly still typical of Leitch's work: there were two tiers of seating under cover, and the beam that supported the upper tier had painted diagonal bracing. This one feature alone became Leitch's trademark. The bracing was coincidentally nearly always painted blue to match the team's colours, except at Sunderland, where red was used, of course.

In the centre of each stand's roof Leitch usually placed a small gable or similar device to offer an architectural presence towards the pitch, but at Ibrox this feature became a castellated press box, which has now disappeared to make way for the new roof structure.

Rather like a 19th-century railway station, where the hotel facing the street represented architecture and the train shed engineering, the Ibrox stand is 'engineering' facing the pitch and 'architecture' facing the street. Just as at Fulham's Craven Cottage, and Blackburn's Ewood Park, the Ibrox stand has an architectural public face of ornamental red brick, and a sumptuous interior.

The tenacity of the Leitch approach to stand design is demonstrated by the fact that, when Plymouth Argyle rebuilt its war-damaged ground in the 1950s, it erected a virtual replica of a Leitch stand, but this was the last of the type to be built. The main drawback of this very conventional approach to engineering was that it needed supports at its front edge, which meant that the view of the pitch could often be obscured.

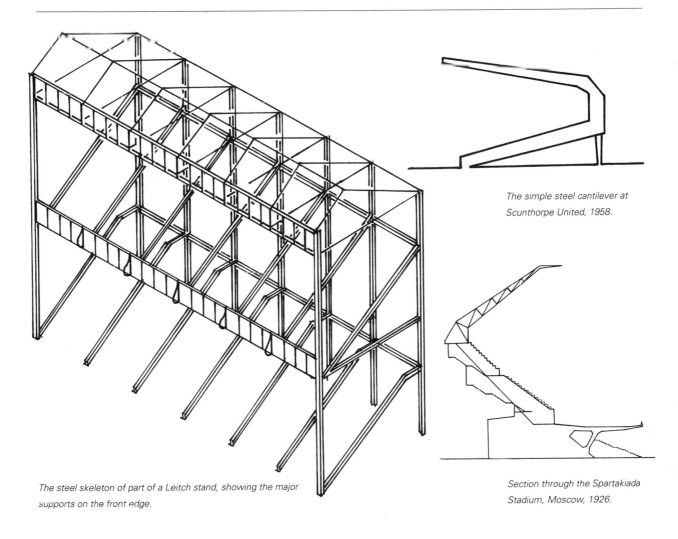

The steel skeleton of part of a Leitch stand, showing the major supports on the front edge.

The simple steel cantilever at Scunthorpe United, 1958.

Section through the Spartakiada Stadium, Moscow, 1926.

The solution to this problem lay in the much more innovative cantilever stand, in which the roof projects horizontally without supports on its outer edge; the tendency to topple is resisted by strong restraints behind the 'fulcrum', or pivoting point. The design of the Spartakiada Stadium in Moscow of 1926 proposed an early and very audacious cantilever. In 1958, on a much more modest scale, Scunthorpe United FC erected Britain's first cantilever stand, in which the covering roof had no support other than at the rear. This was followed in 1961 by the spectacular north stand at Sheffield Wednesday, which used the same principle. Chelsea's three-tier east stand of the late 1970s, which replaced an earlier Leitch structure, was a very expensive and ostentatious state-of-the-art

stand, as far as traditional inner-city British football clubs go.

Simon Inglis, in his definitive book on football ground design, *The Football Grounds of Great Britain* (1987), has commented that Ibrox Park 'is undoubtedly the best club ground of its size in Britain'. One of the reasons for this is that, despite extensive reconstruction, the old south stand has been retained, providing a dignified architectural presence and link with the past. It is now listed.

Leitch's death in 1939 was virtually unnoticed by the architectural establishment, but through the popularity of football, especially through television, his work has been appreciated by a much wider audience.

Jaywick Sands, Clacton 1930

Jaywick Sands, two miles to the east of Clacton in Essex, was – along with Peacehaven near Brighton on the south coast – one of the 'plotland' developments of the inter-war period, which provoked a strongly negative reaction and gave impetus to the introduction of **planning** legislation.

A huge tract of low-lying marsh and grazing land next to the sea at Jaywick had been acquired by the developer Frank Stedman in 1928 with the aim of developing it through the construction of permanent homes. Advertising for Jaywick Sands talked of generous landscaping, with a 'great lake' and sports facilities. It was supposed to be a 'seaside **garden suburb**', with substantial houses, and it was promoted vigorously in the London press.

But there were problems from the start. The authorities refused to connect the first new homes to the drains, so Stedman settled for constructing 'beach huts' instead, with Elsan toilets that had to be emptied daily. The local council then objected, claiming that many people were living permanently in these 'huts', which in some cases had six rooms.

Jaywick was becoming a settlement of small chalets, and its occupants were making the trip out from London each weekend. Like Peacehaven, Jaywick was primarily designed for the motor car. Even some of the roads, like Austin Avenue, were named after makes of car.

There was a good spirit of community and organization amongst the pre-war settlers. They described themselves as 'just one big happy family'. Yet they were forever battling with the local council to get themselves recognized as a proper residential area, even though they were paying the full rates. One thing they were always demanding was adequate protection from rising water and flooding. Their homes were continually getting waterlogged, and in 1953 a violent flood left 35 of the 400 or more residents dead.

An attempt in the 1970s to buy out the old chalets and knock them down failed, and many still remain. Jaywick has now evolved into a more permanent suburban development, and it enjoys full recognition by its local council. The sewers were finally laid in the 1980s. But now, instead of being populated by weekend escapers from London in their motor cars, most of the residents are retired people.

Despite the layout of the roads, Jaywick's appear-

Planning

Planning as we know it today was only really established in the Town and Country Planning Act of 1932. This Act required local authorities to declare what sort of development they thought should take place throughout their areas of jurisdiction. They drew up planning schemes for these areas, which were then sent to central government for consultation and approval. Even more important than the 1932 Act was the Town and Country Planning Act of 1947, which introduced the concept of planning permission and the right of local authorities to exert control over the aesthetics of proposed developments.

One of the most important aspects of planning legislation is the effect it has on the value of property and land: a piece of land that is zoned for, say, housing is bound to be worth more than a similar piece of land zoned for agriculture. The 1932 Act tried to deal with this by offering 'compensation' to owners whose land was devalued due to the implementation of planning schemes, and demanding 'betterment' from owners whose land had increased in value.

After the Second World War the amount that the community at large benefited from betterment depended very much on the political party in power. The right of local authorities to say what goes on in their areas has also changed with the political tide. Socialist governments since

the war have tended to give great power to local authorities to control development; Conservative governments have tended to give many more powers to developers, regardless of the views of the local authority. Under the Conservative adminstration of the 1980s and 90s a developer has the power to appeal to the central government against a decision by a local authority, and if the government finds against the local authority, the developer is allowed compensation.

Not only have local authorities tried over the years to determine what sort of development takes place, they have also tried to vet the architectural quality of that development. This 'aesthetic control' has been actively opposed by architects, who resent planners trying to get involved in the business of building design. But it could be argued that planners are more sensitive to what is acceptable to the population at large than architects are.

ance is that of an undisciplined, almost ramshackle development (although the residents would resent such a description). It would certainly be impossible for such developments to take place now. The planning laws have evolved radically since the early 1930s, and the running battle the residents fought with bureaucracy from the start is proof that Jaywick was deeply resented by the powers that be.

In the 1970s a number of architectural academics, inspired by the studies of **Robert Venturi** *et al.* in Las Vegas, began to take the folk-art forms of Jaywick Sands seriously. To them the owner-applied ornamentation seemed evidence of a 'popular culture' in architecture. And if, as the Las Vegas study implied, it was the job of architecture to communicate messages of homeliness or security, then the study of this popular language should begin in places like Jaywick. Hence busloads of architectural students descended on the place, half loving and half loathing it.

Perhaps the residents are used to this sort of patronizing. The architecture of their chalets is, after all, no less valid a subject of serious study than any other.

Garden suburb

This term was first used to describe the Bedford Park suburb in west London. See p. 64, illustration in North Harrow Estate, 1925

Suburbia

See 51–57 Ivydale Road 1900; Rushby Mead, 1911; North Harrow Estate, 1925; Chelmer Village, 1974

Robert Venturi

See Aztec West, 1987

The settlement of small chalets at Jaywick Sands was 'just one big happy family'.

Wicklands Avenue, Saltdean 1934

High and Over, Amersham:
Amyas Connell, 1929.

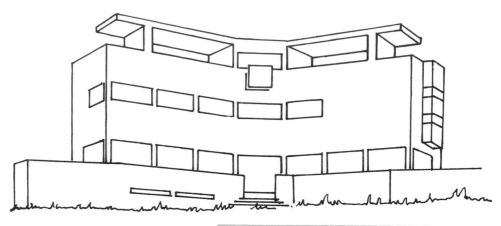

The De La Warr Pavilion, Bexhill-on-Sea:
Erich Mendelsohn and Serge
Chermayeff, 1936.

Maison La Roche, Paris:
Le Corbusier,
1924 (from Towards a New
Architecture, *1927).*

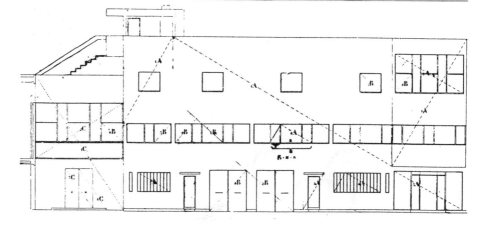

In the 1930s the south-coast resort towns became showcases for the new International Style that had recently been imported from Continental Europe. Undoubtedly the most famous British building in the style is the De La Warr Pavilion at Bexhill-on-Sea, which was designed by a pair of German immigrant architects, **Erich Mendelsohn** and Serge Chermayeff. They had flown from Nazi Germany and practised together in Britain until 1936, when Mendelsohn moved to the USA, but not before they, and other émigrés such as Walter Gropius, would help to consolidate the **Modern movement** in Britain.

Of the British architects who pioneered the new aesthetic, Amyas Connell, Basil Ward and Colin Lucas were among the leaders. Their architectural practice was based on the design of exclusive homes for the wealthy – not on the mass-housing projects for which the new architecture was supposed to be best suited.

Back in the late 1920s Connell had designed a house called High and Over at Amersham in Buckinghamshire, which has been claimed to possess 'the first unequivocally modern exterior' in the country. What this meant was that all of its external surfaces were starkly planar, with all decoration and details like window sills kept to a minimum. The windows themselves were horizontal, rather than vertical, in their orientation, and framed with metal, as opposed to timber. The building was, superficially at least, more of a machine than a house. It clearly owed much to the works of **Le Corbusier**, who had not only built prolifically in France, but who had also published much theoretical work, justifying the new architecture. Le Corbusier had shown how the clean, uncluttered lines of passenger ships and aeroplanes were also suitable for buildings, and he had coined the legendary phrase that a house is '*une machine à habiter*' ('a machine for living in').

Le Corbusier's houses were truly magnificent spatial experiences that dispensed entirely with all of the old assumptions about corridors and enclosed rooms. They exploited the notion of the **'open plan'** to the full. By contrast, High and Over is really just a traditional house, dressed up in fashionable new clothes. There are corridors, enclosed rooms complete with fire-

*Revolutionary and new: sketch by Erich Mendelsohn for a 'Pleasure Pavilion', 1920. See also **Peter Jones, 1935** and **The Odeon, 1935**.*

Open plan

While architects were learning how to turn the façades of buildings into thin sheets of glass (see **Peter Jones, 1935**), they were also discovering that the interiors of buildings could be planned as free-flowing spaces, instead of a series of separate, fully enclosed rooms. This was made possible by the use of the structural frame to hold the building up, instead of the walls. As the external walls of the building disappeared, so too did the internal walls. They just became screens, which could be positioned exactly according to taste. This new freedom of the interior was called the 'open plan', or as Le Corbusier called it, the '*plan libre*' or 'free plan'.

Le Corbusier
See Templewood School, 1949; Alton West Estate, 1959; Crown Offices, 1980
Erich Mendelsohn
See Peter Jones, 1935 and The Odeon, 1935

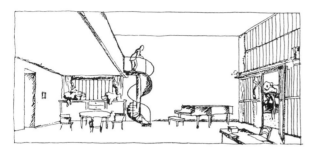

Project for a 'Mass Production House': Le Corbusier, 1921 (from Towards a New Architecture, 1927).

One of the 'machines for living in' on Wicklands Avenue.

Ocean Hotel, Saltdean: R. W. H. Jones, 1938.

places, and all of the trappings of genteel living.

Some four years later after the construction of High and Over, Connell, Ward & Lucas turned their attention to the design of a proposed development of much smaller homes beside the sea at Saltdean, just to the east of Brighton. Only three houses were built – at Wicklands Avenue – though many more were proposed originally. Once again, everything about their interiors was cosy and conventional. It was on the exterior that the houses carried the imagery of the machine aesthetic, with the obligatory white walls devoid of decoration, metal-framed windows and, of course, the roof patio with its flat canopy.

What eventually happened to these three houses is, in a sense, the story of what eventually happened to the Modern movement in Britain. One burnt down, and the two surviving houses were lovingly altered by successive owners, who modified the original 'machine for living in' until it was altogether more comfortable and familiar. All around the houses in Wicklands Avenue there grew up a seaside suburb of much more traditionally designed homes. To visit it all today is a pleasantly piquant experience.

Four years after the Connell, Ward & Lucas houses were built, an architect called R. W. H. Jones gave Saltdean the Ocean Hotel and its Lido. The hotel, just at the end of Wicklands Avenue, is a modern ocean liner run aground. It has the glazed spiral staircases of the Bexhill pavilion, but it looks ponderously symmetrical on its hillside site. The Lido is much more exciting and streamlined, but again typically British – restrained and symmetrical.

There is much more to see in the area: Saint Dunstan's School for the Blind is another modern liner on a hillside site a little closer to Brighton. And in the town itself the very influential Modernist Wells Coates, who was close to the German émigrés, built Embassy Court in 1936 – the first element of an unrealized scheme to redevelop the entire seafront with similar Modernist blocks.

The Modern movement

By the 1930s the effects of the Modern movement and the International Style were being seen in urban Britain. This Modern revolution was not confined to architecture – it had already asserted itself in painting, literature, the theatre and even the cinema. But in architecture it became truly public, all-pervasive and enduring.

'Modern architecture' was both a philosophical programme and a style. To this day, architects calling themselves Modernists flit between philosophy and style so skilfully that it is difficult to see where one begins and the other ends. Philosophically, the Modern movement was revolutionary: it held that architecture should have nothing to do with the past, reflecting only the present day, with its new construction techniques and social aspirations. But any time is, in its own eyes, modern. Some of the late-19th-century architecture of the **arts and crafts** movement was thought at the time to be revolutionary, even if today's observers see it as being steeped in tradition. What was new in the 1920s and 30s was this rejection of the past. As the German Bruno Taut put it in 1920: 'Smash the shell-lime Doric, Ionic and Corinthian columns, demolish the pinheads. Down with the "respectability" of sandstone and plate-glass, in fragments with the rubbish of marble and precious wood. To the garbage heap with all that junk!'

As well as being new, the Modern movement also wanted to be honest and to have nothing to do with the illusion of 'façadism'; it should use building materials frankly and be true to the building's function – a shed should be a shed, and should not be dressed up to look like anything else. This doctrine of honesty and rationality was not new. As early as 1753 the great French theoretician Abbé Laugier had claimed that 'the artist must be able to justify by reasons everything that he does', and in the following century the theoretician Viollet-le-Duc had called for all architecture to be true to its requirements and to its construction.

It is all very well for architecture to be new, of its time, true and rational – but what is it going to look like? To the Modern mind, visual qualities had to come from pure, geometrical forms and colours, and above all the way that these forms create SPACE. The undisputed master of this spatial and sculptural aspect of Modern architecture was the Swiss architect Le Corbusier (Charles Édouard Jeanneret). His influential book *Vers une Architecture* (1923) was translated in 1927 as *Towards a New Architecture*, and it had an immediate effect. It alarmed traditionalists, who complained of its cosmopolitanism and the similarity of its buildings to 'fish tanks'. Sir Reginald Blomfield wrote in the *Listener* in 1933 that the new architecture 'is essentially

Continental in its origin and inspiration, and it claims as a merit that it is cosmopolitan. As an Englishman, and proud of his country, I detest and despise cosmopolitanism'. But the new style inspired Modernists to imitate its sleek white forms, with their flat roofs and horizontal bands of windows.

Occasionally the early manifestations of the British Modern movement were inspired: look at the Burnham-on-Crouch Yacht Club (Joseph Emberton, 1931); the Boots Factory at Beeston, Nottingham (Owen Williams, also 1931 – see **Pioneer Health Centre, 1935**); private houses by Amyas Connell (later Connell, Ward & Lucas) from 1930 onwards; and the work of Tecton, including London Zoo's Penguin Pool (1934) and Highpoint Flats (1935). But usually British Modernism had little to do with the honest expression of new materials, or of the exciting spatial relationships of pure forms. All too often it became exactly what it purported not to be: a style. It became a way of dressing a building up just as traditional decoration had done. And, when sophisticated techniques of system building and prefabrication were developed in the 1960s and 70s (see **Aylesbury Estate, 1977**), the huge and impersonal forms that were built were justified as Modern architecture. Their lack of popularity did much to turn public opinion away from what had, in the 1930s, been such a heroic idea.

Arts and crafts movement
See Boundary Street Estate, 1895
Modern architecture
See Battersea Power Station, 1934; Pioneer Health Centre, 1935; Templewood School, 1949; Alton West Estate, 1959; Alpha House, 1962

Battersea Power Station, London 1934

Battersea Power Station has been called a 'Cathedral of Electricity'. Very few buildings have been able to appeal to the popular consciousness as much the huge four-chimneyed structure on the opposite bank of the River Thames from fashionable Pimlico. Its style has been described as 'jazz modern', but that is not particularly illuminating. There are very few buildings – perhaps only Tower Bridge and the Royal Liver Building in Liverpool can equal it – that have acquired such a memorable public image, while being so ignored by the architectural establishment.

Up until the 1980s London's riverside was lined with power stations. At Greenwich, Bankside, Battersea, Chelsea and Fulham the vast buildings received consignments of coke from river barges, and belched smoke into the atmosphere, sending power both to the domestic consumer and to London's Underground system.

At Battersea, which was really intended to be two power stations side by side in the same building, the internal layout dictated that chimneys should be placed at the corners, leading to the appearance of an upside-down table. Work began on the site in 1929, and the western half of the station was complete in 1934. The later eastern half was completed in 1955. It only required one chimney, so a fourth false chimney was added to maintain the scheme's symmetry.

The London Power Company, which commissioned the scheme, only decided to make use of the services of architects late in the design process. These were Halliday & Agate, whose sumptuous interiors were perhaps more suitable to cinema foyers than power stations. The opulent control room, with its huge swivelled bakelite ammeters, was like a science-fiction fantasy. But Halliday & Agate's original exterior designs were less convincing. The sheer volume of the building demanded that it should be built with a steel frame, and then clad with a skin of brickwork. It was, after all, just a giant shed.

The acclaimed architect Giles Gilbert Scott was called upon to make improvements. His reputation had been built on the designs for Liverpool's Anglican Cathedral and the Cambridge University Library, and – perhaps the most well-known design by any British architect the red telephone kiosks for the General Post Office. None of these designs could be described as being aggressively modern. Scott hated the sort of Modernism that was just beginning to establish itself in Britain in 1930, claiming that the Modern movement 'suffers . . . from a certain shallowness and superficiality;

A K6 telephone kiosk, designed by Giles Gilbert Scott.

Battersea Power Station: the turbine hall of the first phase, after having been stripped out.

Bankside Power Station, 1936.

it lacks quality' and that 'this modernist movement . . . prescribes the same austerity and bleak absence of ornament for all buildings'. He much preferred the idea of a **Modern architecture** that was rich in detail and not quite so negative in its attitude to ornament.

But the scope for architectural modelling at Battersea was very limited. Scott's only opportunity for introducing detail lay in the the vast brick walls and the chimneys that were to stand at each corner. These were designed skilfully: great care was taken in working out how the chimneys sat on their brick bases, and much detail was introduced at the top of the walls. The massive band of grooves at the top of the building was an inspired way of emphasizing its bulk, while at the same time making it appear a familiar to the popular eye through the use of a conventional motif. It is almost an entablature, straight out of classical architecture. As Scott wrote: 'The pendulum will swing back to a proper balanced view of sparse ornament, beautiful in its design and placed just where it is needed and nowhere else. Contrast between plain surfaces and sparse well-placed ornament can produce a charming effect.'

The last of London's great brick power stations, at Bankside, was completed in 1960, with Scott once again acting as consultant architect. Fired by oil, it has just one central chimney, and is even grander in scale and detail than Battersea.

Once they had ceased to generate electricity, both power stations suffered controversy over their future re-use. Battersea was to become a leisure park, but the initiative failed; Bankside is to become an art gallery. Yet even if these great buildings helped to turn the industrial shed into architecture, it needs more than this historical achievement to justify keeping them. Certain questions need to be asked. Is there a social benefit in doing so? Are the buildings worth saving in any case? And, perhaps most important of all – who says so?

Modern architecture
See Wicklands Avenue, 1934; Pioneer Health Centre, 1935; Templewood School, 1949; Alton West Estate, 1959; Alpha House, 1962

Pioneer Health Centre, London 1935

Set deep in the suburbs of Peckham, which by the 1930s were already in decline (see **51–57 Ivydale Road, 1900**), the Pioneer Health Centre was an innovation in community health care, and – with its concrete frame and large areas of glazed wall – in construction.

During the 1930s many middle-class intellectuals set about 'discovering' working-class society. Experiments in 'mass observation' took place, and the arts – cinema, photography and literature – all reflected an interest in the less fortunate sections of society. Scientists also began to take an interest: a pair of doctors based in Peckham wanted to test their theories that health care in the inner city should be about preventing sickness, and not just curing it. It was quite clear that the health of the community in these areas was very poor, and this was not just due to the well-known diseases, but also to less tangible factors like stress, diet and housing conditions.

The resultant health centre, which was originally set up in an old house in 1926, offered regular check-ups to whole families, who paid a small membership fee, and gave the doctors the chance to observe family members and test whether their theories were correct. Before long, the doctors had established that most health problems were not just going to be cured by regular check-ups. What was needed was a new centre that did not just take care of people's health, but was also a place where they could enjoy themselves, with a bar and a place for dancing.

The engineer Owen Williams designed the new Pioneer Health Centre, which was opened in 1935. The site chosen in Peckham was fortunate because it allowed a lot of open space to be left in front of the building, where it was hoped that outdoor social activities could take place. The building was based on a **reinforced-concrete** frame, with concrete floors supported on square columns with mushroom-shaped tops. The façade that faces the road is almost entirely built in glass, in six gently curving bay windows, so that as much light as possible can penetrate the main social spaces inside.

Beneath these windows on the ground floor, the glazing could be removed, providing an open space for children to play. At the core of the building's plan is an Olympic-sized swimming pool, which is entered at first-floor level. Daylight is everywhere, and the atmosphere inside the building is one of openness, which suited the founders' aims perfectly. The Health Centre was a very modern building for its time, and was quickly acclaimed for both its social and its structural innovations.

In one respect, though, the Health Centre is not innovative – its symmetrical plan and façade belong to the classical tradition. But then, as we have seen at **Wicklands Avenue, 1934**, the British architectural establishment never fully accepted all the possibilities of **Modern architecture** that had been exploited on the Continent.

Nor did the architectural establishment fully accept Williams, and it has been suggested that this was because he was not a qualified architect. Qualified or not, Williams produced a design for the vast Boots Factory at Beeston, Nottingham (completed in 1937), that has been widely acclaimed as a fine pioneering piece of Modern architecture. Like the building at Peckham, it supports its upper floors on a grid of mushroom-shaped columns. It is surrounded on all sides by full-height glazing, interrupted only on the façade by the intermediate floors.

Sadly the Pioneer Health Centre had to close when war broke out, and the families that used it were evacuated. But the building still remains, and it is still performing something close to its original function for the local education authority.

Modern architecture

See Wicklands Avenue, 1934;
Battersea Power Station, 1934;
Templewood School, 1949;
Alton West Estate, 1959; Alpha
House, 1962

Reinforced concrete

See Lion Chambers, 1905

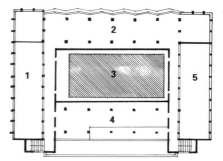

1 gym
2 main hall
3 pool
4 cafeteria
5 theatre

First-floor of the Pioneer Health Centre. Left: swimmimg pool; right: plan (notice the symmetrical organization).

Peter Jones, London 1935

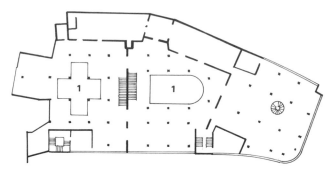

First-floor plan of Peter Jones.   **1 light wells to floor below**

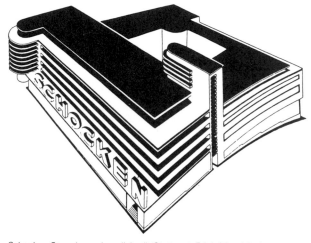

Schocken Store (now demolished), Stuttgart: Erich Mendelsohn, 1926.

Detail of the curtain wall at Peter Jones.

When he designed the Peter Jones store in Sloane Square, Chelsea, William Crabtree was a very young man straight out of university. He had just completed his final student's design for a large store in Oxford Street, and it was through this that he was introduced to Spedan Lewis, the founder of the John Lewis Partnership, who was convinced that the old buildings at Sloane Square needed replacing.

While researching for the new Peter Jones project, Crabtree visited Germany and studied the work of **Erich Mendelsohn**. In the late 1920s Mendelsohn had built a number of stores for the Schocken chain, whose modern exteriors were vigorous in design and acted as advertisements in their own right. But Crabtree was equally impressed by a Berlin office block of Mendelsohn's: the ten-storey Columbushaus of 1931 had a façade that gently curved along the edge of the street. The elegant modulation of the curved horizontal window bands could provide a simple and powerful architectural statement; entirely appropriate for the King's Road frontage of Peter Jones, which also curved gently.

But the new design also had to contend with the London Building Acts, which, until they were eventually replaced by the national Building Regulations in 1985, very strictly governed the standards of construction in the capital. These Acts not only limited the height of a new building, but they also required its façade to be fireproof. Crabtree's first job was to interpret these Acts in such a way that complied with them as well as enabling the new store to approach the elegance of Mendelsohn's work.

Lewis had insisted that the new store should have generous open areas inside, where fabrics could be displayed in natural light. To enable this, the structural frame was designed with long spans in between the columns, so that the internal walls could be planned freely, providing the flexibility that is essential for effective retailing. Only the thick fire-resistant walls and their shutters interrupt the spacious plan. In the centre of the store large light wells were provided, for which the supporting columns were set back a good distance, giving the impression of weightlessness.

On the street façade Crabtree employed a **curtain wall** – one of the first examples of its use in Britain. Unlike in a conventional building, where the wall is a part of the building's structure, a curtain wall has no structural function at all. It is simply a screen clipped onto the edges of the floors. The structural columns that support these floors are set well back from the edge of the building, so that the façade is genuinely 'free': it can conform to any shape and have any amount of windows in it. This ability to have a fully glazed wall is particularly useful in a department store, especially for the ground-floor display windows, and this was exploited to the full at Peter Jones.

In the upper floors the curtain wall was made from glazed panels supported on pressed-steel mullions, which were then covered with bronze facings. Pilkington, the glass manufacturer, had given much assistance in the development of the façade system, regarded as sufficiently revolutionary for a small 'dry run' to be erected on a building in nearby Cadogan Gardens.

Seen from Sloane Square, the term 'curtain wall' makes a lot of sense, for the façade curves gently down Kings Road in a most light and graceful way. At the top of the building the accommodation is set back, partly to comply with the Building Acts. There was originally intended to be a swimming pool and sun lounge up there, but these ideas were later abandoned. Even so, the smooth walls and railings of the top storeys very eloquently suggest the design of ocean liners.

The contrast with **Selfridges, 1907** is profound. The two buildings are in the same line of business, and yet they both use utterly different architectural approaches in a conscious attempt to appeal to their customers. If Selfridges speaks of quality and tradition, Peter Jones broadcasts chic progress. But much more importantly, as far as the eventual acceptance of Modern architecture as the way of designing urban buildings was concerned, Peter Jones was also a very economical building indeed for its type, and money is more persuasive than any fashion.

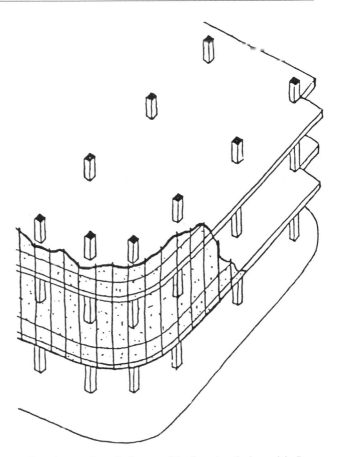

Peter Jones: schematic diagram of the 'free elevation', as originally printed in a contemporary edition of the Architectural Review.

The workshop block of the Bauhaus building in Dessau, Germany: Walter Gropius, 1925.

Curtain wall
Trace the evolution of the fully glazed façade from Oriel Chambers, 1864 and Lion Chambers, 1905, on to Willis, Faber & Dumas, 1975
Erich Mendelsohn
See Wicklands Avenue, 1934 and The Odeon, 1935
Stores
See also Selfridges, 1907; Milton Keynes Central, 1979; Meadowhall, 1990

The Odeon, Weston-super-Mare 1935

In 1920 Oscar Deutsch moved from the family scrap metal business in Birmingham into cinema management. Ten years later he opened the first Odeon cinema at Perry Barr in Birmingham .

These were times of rapidly growing popularity for the cinema, and extravagant use of architectural detail was employed to create a fantasy atmosphere for the buildings both externally and, more especially, internally. The 1930s saw the rise of the Granada chain, with its decorative and exotic interiors, of which the Granada cinema in Tooting is the most famous, with its vast foyers (one a 'hall of mirrors') and its auditorium resplendent in gold-covered decoration that exploits every permutation of Gothic, from 13th-century France to 15th-century Venice.

These were also the years of the 'atmospheric' cinemas which, based on the huge 6000-seat auditoria in the USA, attempted to create the illusion that the audience was sitting in the open air – evoking, for example, an Italian garden, among the Lombardy poplars, or a Moorish town.

The Odeon chain was not so sumptuous. Deutsch believed that the best way to operate in a highly competitive business was to build a cinema in the high street of every town with a population of over 25 000 people. Key to the success of the operation was to give the exterior of the cinemas an instantly recognizable house style, which not only allowed for standardization and cheapness in construction, but also enabled the Deutsch cinemas to enter the public consciousness. (ODEON wittily became known as Oscar Deutsch Entertains Our Nation.)

In 1934 Deutsch opened his latest new cinema in Warley. T. Cecil Howitt, the architect of the Weston-super-Mare Odeon, designed the exterior, while the interior was created by a team that included the architect Harry Weedon. This was the start of a long and profitable relationship between Deutsch and Weedon. Weedon not only went on to design many more of the chain's cinemas, but he also advised Deutsch on designs commissioned from other practices. By 1937, with over 300 cinemas constructed for the chain, the pace in Weedon's office was frantic. David Atwell, in his book *Cathedrals of the Movies* (1980), relates how Weedon had given his chief assistant 12 hours' notice to travel 100 miles to survey a new site, and then just a week to develop the outline design.

Each local site brought its own challenges for the designer: a cinema is after all just a huge shed which needs a public façade to act as advertisement and a

The 'Egyptian' façade of the 2500-seat Carlton in London's Essex Road: George Coles, 1930. It is now a bingo club.

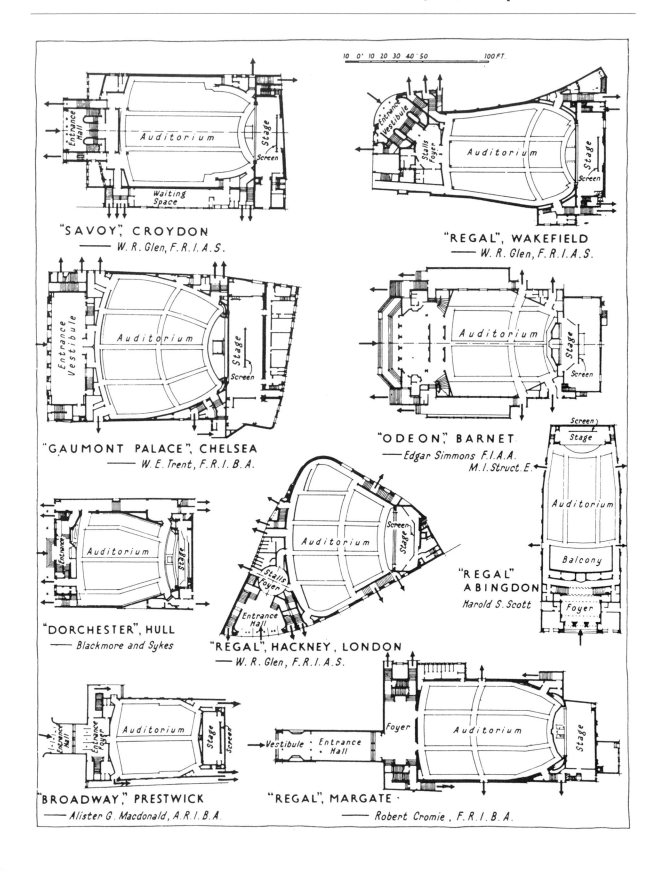

10 0' 10 20 30 40 50   100 FT.

"SAVOY", CROYDON
—— W. R. Glen, F. R. I. A. S.

"REGAL", WAKEFIELD
—— W. R. Glen, F. R. I. A. S.

"GAUMONT PALACE", CHELSEA
—— W. E. Trent, F. R. I. B. A.

"ODEON", BARNET
—— Edgar Simmons F. I. A. A.
M. I. Struct. E.

"DORCHESTER", HULL
—— Blackmore and Sykes

"REGAL", HACKNEY, LONDON
—— W. R. Glen, F. R. I. A. S.

"REGAL" ABINGDON
Harold S. Scott

"BROADWAY," PRESTWICK
—— Alister G. Macdonald, A. R. I. B. A.

"REGAL", MARGATE
—— Robert Cromie, F. R. I. B. A.

good number of emergency exits leading from the auditorium. The shape of the site will determine where these key elements are placed. Once these problems had been addressed, the office could draw on all its standardized designs: for example, Weedon had developed six variations of layout for auditorium seating that were able to satisfy all the planning regulations of different local authorities.

The architectural corporate image that was established for the Odeon chain was based on a number of influences, especially the Berlin cinemas of the 1920s, including the Universum Cinema designed by **Erich Mendelsohn** in 1926. In addition, there were strong references to the art deco style – also of the 1920s – and Deutsch's wife personally supervised much of the cinemas' interior design within this idiom. The main façades, with their elegant curves and Modern horizontal bands of windows, were faced with faience or Carraware, which was a popular and cheap commercial product. A 1937 advertisement for Carraware showed two Odeons declaring that the material is

'available in several delicate shades . . . Cinema designers . . . fully realise that such a building should attract the passer-by through appearance as well as by its programmes. Many designs use Carraware in cream-glazed slab form for the main frontage, with bands of the ware in other colours, as a contrast. By night, such a combination forms an excellent background for neon and other forms of lighting – an important point where cinemas are concerned.'

The stylized 'elephant's trunk' motif dominating the façade of the one-time Odeon in Rayners Lane, Harrow: F. E. Bromige, 1935.

Erich Mendelsohn
See Wicklands Avenue, 1934
and Peter Jones, 1935

(Left) Comparative plans of 1930s cinemas.

Prefabricated Dwellings 1946

Between 1905 and 1908 three exhibitions were held to show off ways that houses could be built employing 'non-traditional' methods of construction. Most common were techniques using concrete blocks and panels, but on the whole these did not entice the building industry to abandon its traditional methods.

Following the First World War the government actively sponsored alternatives to traditional house construction, promoting both steel and concrete systems. In 1925 the 'Airey' home was developed by a manufacturer of precast concrete, using small concrete panels that were clipped into a frame. Over 12 000 houses were built in this way, and many still survive, almost indistinguishable from more traditionally built houses.

During the Second World War serious consideration was once again given to non-traditional forms of construction, and to the prefabrication of houses in particular. In 1944 the prime minister, Winston Churchill, launched the Temporary Housing Programme, with the aim of building hundreds of thousands of temporary homes based on a steel-frame construction.

The most successful of the temporary home designs was developed by a consortium of aircraft manufacturers calling themselves AIROH (Aircraft Industries Research Organization for Housing). Their aluminium bungalow design became the model of the 'prefab', and 54 000 of them were built for housing authorities throughout Britain.

Aluminium, and not steel, was chosen because it was the material used in aircraft construction, even though it was so much more expensive than steel. The government wanted the aircraft industry to produce more than just planes, to ensure the industry's survival once the war was over, so it subsidized the AIROH homes very generously indeed, paying the manufacturer over half the cost of a traditional three-bedroomed house for each bungalow built.

The dwellings were constructed in the factory in four sections, and transported to the building sites on large lorries that had been designed to carry aircraft. The techniques of manufacture had been learned from the very successful 'Liberty Ship' programme of shipbuilding introduced in the USA, in which a full-sized cargo ship took only four days to assemble from prefabricated parts.

In addition to AIROH, the other leading suppliers of

A 'BISF' steel unit, 1948.

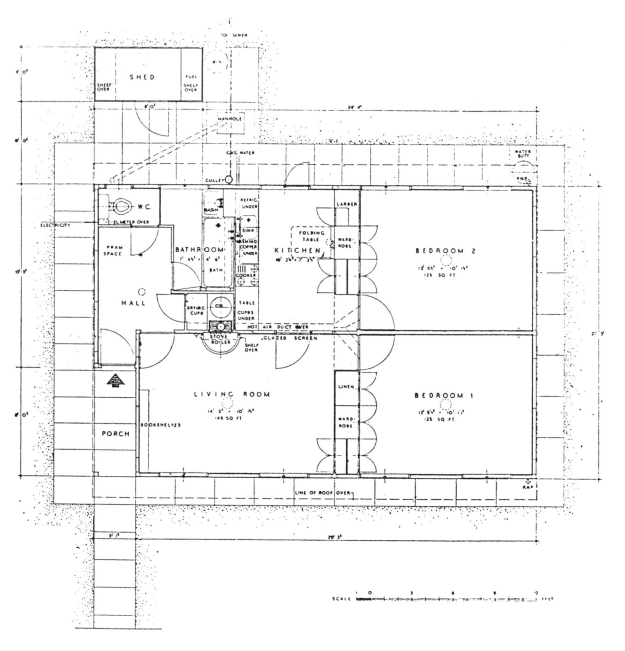

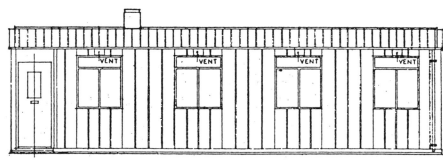

temporary prefabricated houses were Aroon and Uni-Seco, who together supplied nearly 70 000 units.

Another design for a prefab was developed by the government itself and used a steel, as opposed to aluminium, construction. Called the Portal Home after the then Minister of Works, Lord Portal, it was to comprise panels made by Briggs Motor Bodies Ltd which were assembled on site using car-building techniques. 50 000 Portal Homes were commissioned, but the order was cancelled because the wartime steel industry could not spare the raw material.

Many of the temporary homes have survived much longer than was intended, and some remain popular even today, but the prefab construction programme stopped very soon after the end of the war. There was a desperate shortage of construction materials, and the prefabrication of whole houses was simply not as cheap as it was thought it would be: it had been impossible to justify the technique on grounds of cost alone, and each prefab was more expensive to build than a conventional house.

But the concept of prefabrication of smaller building elements like wall panels continued to be put into practice. Airey homes were still being built, and a number of other **building systems** had emerged, such as the rather traditional-looking Cornish unit with its mansard roof, or the BISF unit with its steel construction. The 1960s and 70s witnessed a peak in industrialized housing construction (see **Aylesbury Estate, 1977**), though this was soon to be followed by a rapid decline.

A 'Cornish' concrete unit, 1949.

Building systems
See Templewood School, 1949; Alpha House, 1962; Aylesbury Estate, 1977; Walters Way, 1987

(Left) Plan and elevation of the Portal Home.

Templewood School, Welwyn 1949

Following the end of the Second World War the government raised the school-leaving age, and offered to erect huts to provide the extra classroom space that was needed for the greater number of pupils. This was a time when there was a considerable shortage of traditional building materials and of skilled labour. In view of this, Hertfordshire County Council decided to develop its own, **modular** system for designing permanent new schools, which would use prefabricated components, made in the factory, that would not require such a high level of skilled labour to erect on site.

The first of these schools was built in 1946, and many followed soon afterwards. The design of these buildings was undertaken by teams of architects, who had little scope for individual artistic expression as they had to stick to a system of construction in which all the different details had been worked out beforehand. A government pamphlet of 1949 stated how 'this approach to design and building will lead us . . . to new architecture which is a simple and unselfconscious expression of present-day requirements'.

Templewood School of 1949 is typical of this approach. It shows a marked contrast with traditional school design (see **Primrose Hill School, 1885**). Externally, it is light in appearance, with large windows – required by law to allow a high level of natural light into the building, and made possible by the framed construction system, in which all the load is carried on columns. The building is completely free of the old architectural formulae of symmetry and historically inspired ornamentation, which characterized the design of most pre-war schools. It is unmistakably a piece of **Modern architecture**.

This is most apparent in the planning of the school, in which a much greater emphasis has been placed on the way the interior works than on the external appearance. It is almost as if it was designed from the inside out. The divisions between the various spaces are much less pronounced than in a traditional school: the entrance hall merges into the assembly hall, and the teaching areas are separated from the circulation spaces by movable shutters. This sense of openness, and of flowing space, was one of the hallmarks of the Modern movement.

Along with the great progress that was being made at the same time in housing design by London County Council's architects' department (see **Alton West Estate, 1959**), the Hertfordshire schools were the most widely admired British building type of their period.

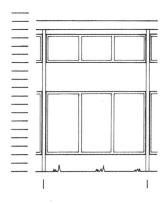

The Hertfordshire system: buildings were divided horizontally into modules of 8 ft 3 in (approx. 2500 mm) and vertically into modules of 8 in (approx. 200 mm).

Modular design

The Hertfordshire schools were designed using a modular system in which all of the sizes of the major building components were standardized. The main steel structural frame was organized on an 8 ft 3 in (approx. 2500 mm) grid on the ground. In other words, columns could only be placed at points where imaginary **grid lines** 8 ft 3 in apart crossed. This module governed the planning of the building, and the size of the rooms was designed to be in multiples of that basic module.

The plan of Templewood School follows this discipline: all of the columns and principal walls are on the 8 ft 3 in grid. The modular system also works vertically, but here the basic module was a much smaller 8 in (approx. 200 mm). This vertical system governed the heights of the windows, and the ceilings and roofs. The reason for adopting this modular system was to enable building components to be standardized, which in turn called for massive co-operation between all the parties involved in the building initiative, from the owners of new buildings to the suppliers of the components. The attempt to modularize design had all the confidence of the immediately post-war period, in which the old traditions were to be replaced by a new, more democratic social fabric. A very active Modular Society was formed, which tried to promote the discipline of modularization throughout

the building industry.
Even **Le Corbusier** developed
his own, highly personal
system, known as 'the Modulor'. This was based, not on
repeating the fundamental
module arithmetically, as the
Hertfordshire system had
been, but on one which
increased geometrically
according to the **golden ratio**.
A number of his buildings
used the method, but it never
caught on to the extent that
he had wanted.
The Segal Method (see
Walters Way, 1987) is also
a modular system, but in this
case its purpose is not to enable lots of buildings to be
built to the same pattern (as
in the Hertfordshire schools),
or to provide a philosophical
discipline to design (as with
Le Corbusier), but to enable
people to construct their own
homes, using 'off-the-shelf'
building materials.

The idea of using a system of construction to build
badly needed buildings in large numbers was clearly
sensible and, in official circles at least, had become
very popular. In 1955 the minister of education commented on how the Hertfordshire schools were 'both
businesslike and beautiful', and two years later the
government, in collaboration with Nottinghamshire
and other education authorities, had established a
very ambitious programme of prefabricated building
design to be applied nationwide.

Called CLASP (the Consortium of Local Authorities
Special Programme), it offered the benefits of bulk pur-
chasing of materials and the pooling of expertise. The
cost of schools and other types of buildings constructed using the CLASP system was comparatively
low, and the resulting designs not unattractive. As in
the Hertfordshire schools, which were its forerunners,
the CLASP system was based on a simple frame upon
which a wide range of prefabricated panels could
be fixed. During the 1960s it was used widely, most
notably for the first buildings of the new York
University.

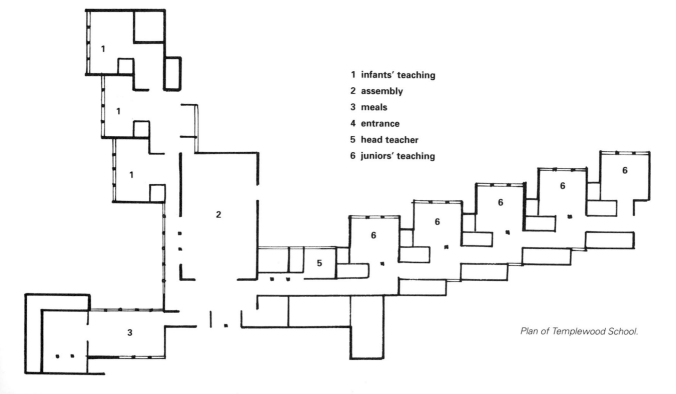

1 infants' teaching
2 assembly
3 meals
4 entrance
5 head teacher
6 juniors' teaching

Plan of Templewood School.

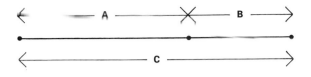

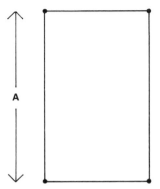

Grid lines

These are imaginary lines used by the building designer to discipline the building's organization. Grid lines are not just restricted to a rigorously modular system, as in the Hertfordshire schools. For example, they helped **Palladio** to design his buildings' plans and elevations. They can also be perceived as the discipline behind the positioning of the structural columns on a number of buildings (see **Peter Jones, 1935** and **Hillingdon Civic Centre, 1977**).

If a straight line is divided according to the golden ratio, the ratio between the small part to the large part is the same as the ratio between the large part and the whole, or B:A = A:C.

Golden ratio

The ratio of 1:1.6180339 has been used throughout the history of building design. It is thought to be the most pleasing ratio possible: the 'golden section' rectangle is regarded as beautiful, as is a straight line divided into the same ratio. Not only is it significant aesthetically, but it is also arithmetically and geometrically very important. It is the only proportion in which the ratio between the small part to the large part is the same as the ratio between the large part and the whole. It can be calculated as follows, using the Fibonnaci series.

Think of any two numbers, and write them down next to each other. To the right of these numbers write a third number that is the sum of the first two numbers. To the right of these three numbers write a fourth that is the sum of the two numbers immediately to its left; then write a fifth that is the sum of the two numbers immediately to its left; and so on. Next, take any number in the series and divide it by the number immediately to its left.

The answer will approach 1:1.6180339 the further along the series you go.

Royal Festival Hall, London 1951

The Festival of Britain was held in 1951, exactly a century after the Great Exhibition, for which the magnificent Crystal Palace was built. The 1951 Festival, while not nearly so revolutionary as its predecessor, was described as a 'tonic to the nation' following the battering Britain had received during the Second World War. These were times of liberal optimism, when the post-war Labour government dreamed of creating a 'Socialist Commonwealth of Britain' – a dream that would sadly remain unfulfilled due to the crippling debts that the country faced in the aftermath of war.

The British public had come to detest the grimy state of its 19th-century buildings, and the Festival was conceived as a showcase of current architectural thinking, suggesting the way that the future might look. However, what became known as the 'Festival Style' did not really represent anything new, but had its roots in the pre-war period when, as we have seen, the British establishment produced its own homely version of Continental Modernism. The Festival was the flowering of 'the acceptable face of **Modern architecture**', and to its critics – who would go on to champion the new **brutalism** – it was too genteel.

Although the Festival was intended to be held throughout Britain, its principal site was on the south bank of the Thames, which for many years had lain derelict. The main architectural features of the Festival site were the 'Shot Tower' – a relic of the past which had been spruced up and given a dish aerial to receive radio signals from space; the 'Dome of Discovery' – a 111 m diameter, round exhibition hall with an aluminium-framed roof; the 'Skylon' – a 100 m 'vertical feature', of which some wag once said 'like Britain, it has no visible means of support'; and the new Royal Festival Hall. This was badly needed, since the old Queen's Hall had been bombed in the war. It would be the only Festival building to be kept, and formed the nucleus for the South Bank arts complex of the 1960s.

The precise site for the concert hall was the old Lion Brewery, which dominated the muddy foreshore with its tall façade and statue of a lion (which still survives at the foot of Westminster Bridge). The design team for the hall was based just down the road, at the **London County Council**, and set to work on a very tight timetable leading up to opening in May 1951. The biggest problem facing the designers was the requirement for a very large auditorium of 3000 people on a very small site. There was seemingly no room for both a large foyer and an auditorium of this size. In the face of this problem, the architects came up with the

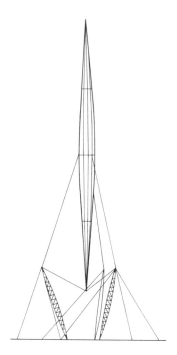

The Skylon, 1951: 'like Britain, it has no visible means of support'. It was actually supported by an imaginative array of tension wires. Like the **Prefabricated Dwellings, 1946**, *the Skylon brought the technology of aeroplane manufacture into the building industry.*

solution that the auditorium would be placed over the foyer, with the access stairs and balconies rising along the sides of the auditorium. It became known as the 'egg-in-the-box' approach: the idea of surrounding the 'egg' (i.e. the auditorium) with 'front-of-house' functions not only enabled much more to be put on to the site, but it also allowed the auditorium to be 'wrapped' in accommodation, which helped its acoustics tremendously.

An auditorium with a capacity of 3000 seats is probably too large for effective acoustics, but the new hall had to bring music to a wide section of society. What's more, every seat had to be able to receive the same quality of sound. This hall was not meant to be a place where all the social classes sat in their own appropriate place, the 'higher' echelons being better seated than the lower: it was a hall for the People.

Perhaps the biggest benefit of the egg-in-the-box solution was the sense of open space that it allowed. On entering the Royal Festival Hall, its openness is immediately apparent: there are views out through the other side of the building, and there are views upwards to its top, through the gaps left between the balconies and the auditorium. Everywhere there are steps, leading up half storeys to other balconies, and

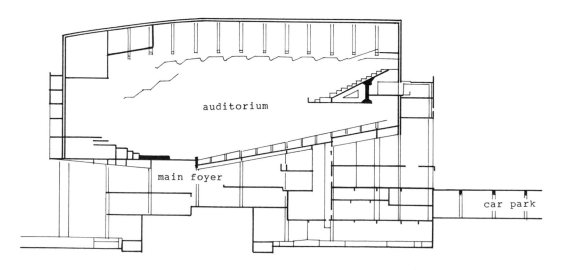

Section of the Royal Festival Hall as first built, showing the auditorium placed over the main foyer. The river frontage (to the right) was later extended.

giving further glimpses to the outside. In the bar area the great sloping ceiling is obviously the underside of the raked auditorium seating above.

Another noteworthy feature of the Royal Festival Hall is the care that was taken in designing even the most humble features. The marble floors, the timber balustrades to the stairs and the famous carpet design are all examples.

Much of the original building has been altered – it was even extended out towards the Thames in 1961 – but its essential quality remains. It is significant to us now not just as a principal concert hall in a very important setting, but also because it symbolizes better than any other building the sense of democracy that pervaded the country after the war. The Royal Festival Hall is one of the most popular buildings in Britain, appreciated both by architects and, more significantly, by the public.

The interior of the Royal Festival Hall beneath the auditorium, with clear views through the building.

The auditorium of the Royal Festival Hall, with its boxes.

Brutalism
See Crown Offices, 1980
London County Council
See Boundary Street Estate, 1895 and Alton West Estate, 1959
Modern architecture
See Wicklands Avenue, 1934

Lower Precinct, Coventry 1957

The air raids of the Second World War destroyed many European urban centres. Some, such as the French towns of Nantes or St Malo, decided to rebuild along the same lines as before, re-creating the appearance of the old towns. In Britain, including Plymouth and the area around St Paul's in London, the opportunity was taken to redevelop comprehensively along modern lines. Perhaps the greatest challenge of all came with the rebuilding of bomb-ravaged Coventry in the 1950s.

Virtually the whole of the city centre had been destroyed by air raids in November 1940, and the redevelopment that followed the end of the war included the construction of the now world-famous St Michael's Cathedral (1951–62), designed by Basil Spence, adjacent to the remains of the old cathedral, which has been kept as a war memorial. The planners devised a system of ring roads and car parks, to eliminate traffic from the new central area. As the city council owned most of the land, it was able to exert great control over the design of the new roads, spaces and buildings.

One of the key elements of the new design was a fully **pedestrianized** shopping precinct, which was begun in 1951, the year of the **Festival of Britain**. The Coventry precinct was, at the time it was built, the largest city-centre pedestrianized area in the country. It was split into two parts, each with two shopping levels: the Upper Precinct to the east was the first to be finished, but it suffered criticism for the poor quality of shopping that it offered. The idea of creating pedestrianized shopping areas was not yet fully understood, and the use of two levels of shopping never worked out as it was intended, for shoppers generally do not like going up to higher levels unless there is a very good reason to do so. This is why later malls like **Meadowhall, 1990** were designed to encourage people to explore the upper levels, by installing exotic lifts rising out of generously planted areas. At the Upper Precinct this was not the case, and as if to underline the area's failure, it has now been comprehensively remodelled.

The later Lower Precinct was more successful. It is separated from the Upper by a pedestrianized cross-street, which now has a completely different aspect from when it was first built. But in the Lower Precinct the slight change in level of the land was cleverly used to ensure that shoppers could get easy access to either level of shops: to pass through the area, they *had* to visit both levels. Despite this, the area is still

Pedestrians and traffic: The Buchanan Report

In response to a growing concern about the way motor traffic was becoming more and more intrusive in the inner city, the government published the **Buchanan Report** in 1963. This was a time when much of the fabric of the inner city was becoming very run down, and the concept of preservation was not at all established. Many great and beautiful structures were demolished, in the confident belief that old buildings should be replaced with new ones in a dynamic and more appropriate style. The Buchanan Report advocated an entirely new approach to building, known as 'traffic architecture'. Its main argument was that cars would be left on roads at ground level, while pedestrians would walk on new high-level streets, without interference from motor traffic. Here is what the report said:

'If buildings and access ways are thought of together, as constituting the basic material of cities, then they can be moulded and combined in all sorts of ways, many of which are more advantageous than the conventional street . . . Although traffic architecture techniques would involve a 'new look' for urban areas, in many ways it could still result in an 'old look' freed from the domination of the motor vehicle . . . the central area of a town might be redeveloped with traffic at ground level underneath a 'building deck' . . . On the deck it would be possible to re-create, in an even better form, the things that have delighted man for generations in towns – the snug, close, varied atmosphere, the narrow alleys, the contrasting open squares, the effects of light and shade, and the fountains and the sculpture.'

The confidence of this modern vision is most evident. In reality, though, it was hardly ever put into practice in the way that was intended. The report went out of its way to say that a lot of money would be needed to make the new pedestrian streets good places to be in – the money was rarely spent.

In London's Covent Garden a grandiose scheme to blitz the area and replace it with a high-level pedestrian route never got further than one building at the north end of Drury Lane. In Lambeth, in south London, a megalomaniac scheme to allow people to walk the 2 km from the town hall to the River Thames at rooftop level never got further than the new Brixton Recreation Centre, whose cut-off, high-level walkways are all that remain of the plan. By the 1980s the doctrine of letting the cars have free rein at ground level, while pedestrians are forced upstairs, had been comprehensively discredited. But there is still no effective answer to how buildings should be designed in relation to traffic.

The Buchanan Report
See also Aylesbury Estate, 1977; Milton Keynes Central, 1979; Ford Estate, 1986
Festival of Britain/Festival style
See Royal Festival Hall, 1951

open to the elements, and its design appears crude in comparison with later, fully enclosed shopping centres.

If the layout of the Coventry precinct is very much of its time, so is its architectural treatment. The Lower Precinct has been described as one of the finest surviving examples of the **Festival style**, and its features do indeed sum up much of British architecture of the 1950s – modern, certainly, but ornamented with motifs that have filtered through the design of the South Bank of 1951. The shallow-pitched canopies over the upper level of shops, the unassuming, almost anonymous treatment of the buildings themselves, and the fussily designed metal balustrades around the edges of the upper walkways are all a mixture of a bold vision of the future, and British homeliness.

The one feature of the Lower Precinct that does demonstrate architectural courage is the round café in the middle, which stands, like the good orthodox Modern building that it is, on a stalk, so that it looks as if it is floating in the air. Originally the Lady Godiva Café, but now a more cosmopolitan burger bar, the café was originally welcomed for its 'sense of display from the upper level . . . especially on winter evenings'.

The optimistic photographs taken when the precinct was new now look very dated. The sun blinds, gay colours and tubs of plants have all gone, giving way to a sad drabness. The city that created it now wants to improve it, saying that 'Lower Precinct is dated' but it is still loved by the architectural intelligentsia, who feel that all their favourite pieces of Modern architecture should be saved, no matter how unpopular they now are.

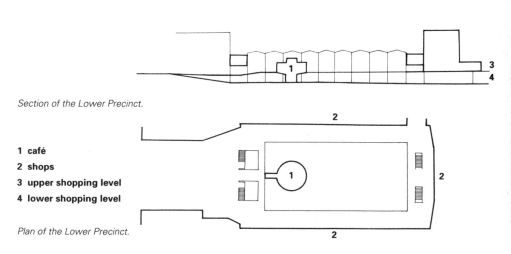

Section of the Lower Precinct.

1 **café**
2 **shops**
3 **upper shopping level**
4 **lower shopping level**

Plan of the Lower Precinct.

Alton West Estate, London 1959

One of the access balconies at Alton West Estate.

When the **London County Council** (LCC) set about building new homes after the Second World War, it did so very energetically. By the middle of 1949, 32 500 new units had been built, but their quality was often criticized.

In the period immediately after the war there were two significant new design developments in high-density housing. One had been the increase in height to over eight storeys, which was made possible by the introduction of lifts, and the other was the increasing use of **prefabrication**, in which large building elements were manufactured off site. But the fundamental policy that high-density **tenement** blocks should be built in the inner city, and that garden city, cottage-type estates would be built out in the suburbs, had remained unchanged since the end of the First World War.

In the early 1950s this old policy began to change, and the new idea of 'mixed development' was introduced. Now, both high-density tall blocks were to be used in the same development as low-density, low-rise cottages. By building some of the blocks high, much more open space was liberated for the benefit of the estate as a whole. The idea of giving as much open space as possible to new housing developments had been established as long ago as at **Boundary Street Estate, 1895**, but it achieved even more impetus from the theoretical proposals of **Le Corbusier**.

His unbuilt 'Ville Contemporaine' (Contemporary City) of 1922 and 'Ville Radieuse' (Radiant City) of 1930 had suggested huge **high-rise** blocks set in green areas. The blocks were all to be lifted off the ground on columns (Le Corbusier called them *'pilotis'*). The advantages of this to a block of flats is difficult to understand, and Le Corbusier's justifications for *pilotis* were mainly aesthetic: they were supposed to symbolize the building's 'liberation from the constraints of the ground', to which traditionally designed buildings had always been tied. The *pilotis* also allowed a clear view of the landscape through to the other side of the building, so that the ground itself became a kind of continuous park. It is known that many members of the LCC's architects department had admired the Ville Radieuse.

Thirty years later, in 1952, Le Corbusier had built the Unité d'Habitation near Marseilles, in which 1600 shipyard workers and their families were housed in just one 20-storey block. The building included shops and community facilities, and access to the flats was from internal 'streets' on every third floor. Doors to flats were arranged on either side of this corridor: some gave access down into flats, while others gave access up. The key to the Unité's design was its section, which could be extended out into any length of block. Again, Le Corbusier's design was raised up on free-standing columns, so that the lowest floor was clear of the ground.

The LCC's Alton West Estate at Roehampton in south-west London was partly modelled on the Unité d'Habitation – *pilotis* and all. The estate was of the 'mixed development' type, in which ten-storey slab blocks were built near to four-storey maisonette blocks.

Implementation of the slab block was not new to the LCC. Even in the early 1950s, and exactly contemporary with the Unité d'Habitation, the ten-storey Bentham Road Estate in Hackney had been built as a slab of undisguised concrete set up on *pilotis*. But at Roehampton the idea was brought much closer to the Le Corbusian ideal by building the blocks into fine open parkland, very different from the Hackney site. The five slabs are of concrete-framed construction, with floors and walls made out of precast units, which have been hoisted into position on to the frame. Each two-storey flat (or maisonette) has access from an external balcony, and each balcony is reached via a staircase and lift zone in the middle of the block.

Very soon after Alton West's construction, the slab block fell out of favour, and for a short while the design of high-density housing was based on the high-rise point block.

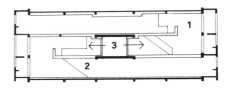

Unité d'Habitation, Marseilles, 1952: enlargement, showing how two-storey maisonettes are arranged around the internal corridor.

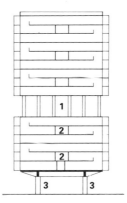

1 **communal facilities**
2 **access corridors**
3 **pilotis**

Unité d'Habitation, Marseilles: section through the block.

Alpha House, Coventry 1962

In the 1960s architects and builders were still struggling to find new techniques for the construction of the ever huger buildings they were being asked to build. Given the pressure on local authorities in such places as Coventry to build **high-rise** blocks, it was hoped at the time that Alpha House would become an acceptable architectural and technical alternative to conventional two-storey house construction.

Technically it was quite innovative: its nickname, 'Jackblock', derives from the fact that it was jacked up, storey by storey, from the ground where it was built. After the foundations had been constructed, 40 hydraulic jacks were put in position on the ground, and the flat concrete roof was cast on top of them. The jacks then lifted the roof up to a storey's height, and what was eventually to be the top floor was built beneath it. This process was repeated for each of the 16 storeys, each floor being assembled out of **precast-concrete** units, and completed right down to the final coat of exterior paint, before being jacked up at a speed of a metre every two hours. In this way all the major building work could be carried out under cover at ground level, and all that was needed to complete the building was the internal fitting-out once the 'jacking' was finished.

Architecturally the building was very much of its day. It stood out conspicuously among its surroundings, and was thought at the time to be a fine piece of design. The façade was 'composed' to form a 'rhythm', which gave it some resemblance to the rhythm of a classical façade. In other words, the window and panel elements provided a strong and basic patterning: black panels alternated with grey, and the whole façade was split into two by a thin white line, which corresponded with the internal walls that divided each of the six flats on each storey.

In this way, the external decoration of Alpha House could reasonably claim to bear a relationship to the function of the building's interior, even though the façade has now been repainted in a more uniform way. This 'honesty' was a very important element of the doctrine of **Modern architecture**, which eschewed wilful decoration. But, like much architecture of its day, Alpha House *is* decorative: it has a style – even if it is for the most part an 'honest' one – and it borrows that style from key buildings of the Modern movement.

Look, for instance, at the way that the lowest part of the building is recessed, and made to look almost invisible. While having no convincing purpose, this

High-rise housing

By the late 1950s there was a great demand for housing. Young married couples were no longer accepting the tradition that they lived with one set of parents until they could afford a home of their own. What was considered a luxury before the war was now an essential, and people looked to their local authorities to provide the new homes. Furthermore, there was a greater demand on space within the home. People could afford more furniture, along with radiograms and refrigerators, and even televisions.

In 1961 the Parker Morris Report from the government laid down generous standards to which all new housing should be designed. Not only was the government committing itself to building new homes as quickly as possible, it was also demanding that those homes should be more spacious than before. In addition, there was pressure to build as many homes as possible on the mininum amount of land or, put another way, to increase the **density**.

As a result, the government put tremendous pressure on local authorities to build high-rise blocks. Since the 1890s, when council housing was conceived, the government has always played a powerful role, by forcing councils to get its permission to build, and by giving out subsidies. In the early 1960s there was a further incentive: the higher the proposed block of flats, the higher the subsidy it would receive for its construction. This in turn made the councils turn to **system-building** techniques.

Yet before the 1960s drew to a close, official policy had been reversed. High-rise or 'point' blocks had been heavily criticized on many grounds – chiefly for shoddy construction – and when the Ronan Point flats collapsed in 1968, following a gas explosion, the high-rise era was brought to an end.

device was highly fashionable, and was employed at **Alton West Estate, 1959** and **Lower Precinct, 1957**. This is what a contemporary critic said of the 'Jackblock': 'The mass of the building seems detached from its base because above the ground floor it is cantilevered from the central core which lies in darkness. Thus the pure lines of the tower can be appreciated without interruption.' In conclusion, the critic commented that 'at the foot of the tower the small buildings huddle almost unobserved . . . only the bright red telephone kiosk provides a note of colour to complement this distinguished building'.

For centuries architecture has changed its values to suit the prevailing technologies and social conditions: at the time Alpha House was built, there was an economic need to build high-rise dwelling blocks. As always, architects and architectural critics obliged by turning it all into art.

Density	See Preston Bus Station, 1969
See Back-to-Back Houses, 1875	**System building**
Modern architecture	See Prefabricated Dwellings, 1946; Aylesbury Estate, 1977;
See Wicklands Avenue, 1934 (main text); Battersea Power Station, 1934; Pioneer Health Centre, 1935; Templewood School, 1949; Alton West Estate, 1959	Walters Way, 1987
	Tenement housing
	See 145 Buccleuch Street, 1892; Boundary Street Estate, 1895; Alton West Estate, 1959; Aylesbury Estate, 1977;
Precast concrete	Mercers House, 1992

Preston Bus Station 1969

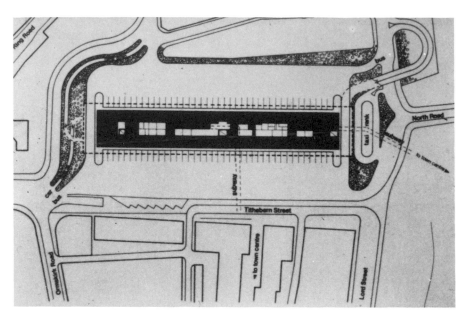

Ground-floor plan of Preston bus station, showing the central 'islands'.

If the Modern movement has all too often been blamed for degrading the streets of urban Britain, perhaps Preston Bus Station and car park – designed by the Building Design Partnership – should remind us that Modern architecture can also be vigorous and, in its own way, very impressive.

It is difficult to disguise the immense bulk of an inner-city car park. Its sides must be open to allow for adequate ventilation, and the need for access ramps defies the logic of conventional architectural formulae. The most common solution has been to create 'traditional' brick walls, with motifs like arches and railings to break up the monotony of such huge masses.

But Preston Bus Station makes no attempt to disguise its function, which is immediately legible from the outside: the lowest parts are a bus station, and the upper parts a car park. Here at last the idea of standing a building on stilts has some logic. The bus station part is a completely glazed box containing all the queuing areas, and the large expanses of glass give waiting passengers a clear view of what is going on outside, so that they are able to pass quickly to waiting buses occupying some of the 80 bays.

More enclosed functions such as ticket offices, snack bars and waiting rooms are placed like islands in the middle of the floor of the bus station. These are,

in effect, like 'buildings within a building' (see **Maidenhead Library, 1973**). Situated above these, a mezzanine, or upper level, accommodates a rest area for the bus crews.

Above the bus station there are the four levels of car-parking decks. Their edges are formed by great upward-sweeping concrete elements that give the whole building a lively and sculptural appearance. The architects chose the curved form because they claimed it was more durable, and able to withstand the weather, than a more conventional vertical surface treatment.

All of these curved edges, and the decks that constitute the interior of the car park, are made of concrete units, which were **precast** in glass-fibre moulds to give a smooth finish, in a factory that was set up specially on site during the construction of the building. The units were each moved into position by crane on to the building's main concrete frame that had been constructed *in situ*. Each of the units is shaped in section like a giant 'T', over 1 m wide and with a central rib to give strength so that it could span 12 m.

One of the most important considerations when designing buildings that use precast concrete sections is the number of moulds that will need to be made, because of the high cost of making them. This is an even more important consideration when the moulds

Interior of Preston Bus Station.

In situ concrete

See Lion Chambers, 1905

Precast concrete

As an alternative to casting the concrete for a building in its final position within the building, or *in situ*, it is also possible to cast it away from its final position, should this be a more convenient solution. This particularly applies when large numbers of reasonably small units are required, like the wall elements of a giant housing estate (e.g. **Aylesbury Estate, 1977**) or the floor beams of a building such as Preston Bus Station/car park.

Once cast, these elements are then lifted into the correct position in the building and fixed in place. Precasting is a cheap and very effective way of making repeated elements such as small window sills and lintels, but it is not advisable when each individual casting needs to be slightly different from the rest. This would require either the shape of the mould to be altered (which is occasionally possible), or the unit to be cut once it has been cast, which risks exposing the metal reinforcement within the unit. Precasting is rarely used for the primary structure of buildings, such as their main frames. These need to have as much strength as possible in all directions, and the joints that would occur when precast units are fixed together would severely weaken them.

are in glass fibre, for they in turn will also need to be moulded, and this process takes time and money.

Preston Bus Station was an ideal candidate for precast units, for it is 150 m long, and the section throughout its length is more or less consistent. The only interruptions to this consistency are the internal ramps enabling cars to move from one level to another, and these needed special moulds. With the exception of these ramp units, each of the main patterns was used over one thousand times during construction, which easily justified the high cost of making the moulds.

This is a building designed to meet the needs of modern transportation, and it looks the part. As we have seen, the ground floor of columns and glass makes perfect sense: the buses nose their way under the car-park overhangs towards the passengers waiting in the comparative warmth of the interior. And true to the requirements of the Modern movement, the four floors above look like nothing other than what they are – a car park.

There may be other ways to design such a huge mass in the middle of a historic town – by giving it a historic veneer, or by putting flats around its edge (as has been done in France), but the Preston building remains a very self-confident assertion of modern architectural values.

Maidenhead Library 1973

Libraries have played a very significant role in the evolution of contemporary architecture. In Paris the Bibliothèque St Geneviève of 1843, designed by Henri Labrouste, introduced a skeleton of slender iron columns and decorative arches into its main reading room. The same architect was called upon to design France's Bibliothèque Nationale in 1865, which again used slender iron columns to support nine domes of faience and glass.

A century later the library at Maidenhead used the latest thinking in steel construction to create a '**space-frame**' over the main reading areas. With a population of around 50 000, Maidenhead required a library that would embrace many more functions than just a book-lending service: in addition to book racks, there had to be a meeting hall, exhibition space and a coffee bar. The architects – Ahrends, Burton & Koralek – responded by creating an atmosphere inside the library that is almost like being in a market hall, with lots of stalls under one main roof.

The lower parts of the library are constructed in brick, and the brick walls weave in and out, quite freely and independently from the roof structure, to form smaller functional spaces as if they were buildings in their own right. Inside, many of the fittings and furnishings are designed as 'pods', so that they can be moved about at will. And above all this happy informality is the great market roof with its latticework space-frame, appearing to have no contact with the walls beneath it.

This idea of placing a 'megastructure' over a complex interior is very modern in conception, creating the same effect of 'buildings within a building' that we saw at **Preston Bus Station, 1969**. The Japanese architect Kenzo Tange also employed a vast space-frame to cover his pavilion at the EXPO in Osaka, 1970.

One critic, writing just after the library had been completed, wrote of 'the dream of placing a sculptured form which is free to bulge outwards or to indent as use requires, inside a translucent shell. We sense in this dream . . . an earthly future akin to that of the Blessed in heaven; in which all the boring, distressing limitations of life are held at bay, in which Man is free to pursue his avocations, unencumbered by fears, ailments or the resisting pressures of the atmosphere.' In other words, the space-frame's roof seems to provide a protective layer against the 'evils' of the outside world: there is something here of the space-age dream of setting up self-contained colonies on other planets.

Space-frames

Space frames, or three-dimensional structural systems, differ from traditional beam or arch construction in one profound way: the structure does not span one point to another in a straight line, but it covers an entire area – like a great latticed plate. This means that huge lightweight roofs can be constructed with the minimum number of columns.

One of the earliest developments of the flat, 3D structure like that at Maidenhead Library was the Mero system, introduced in Germany in the 1940s and still in use today. It relies on a sophisticated 'ball' into which up to 18 steel rods can be screwed to form the 3D lattice. Much larger space-frames were developed in the USA in the 1950s, where the Air Force needed a system for building vast aircraft hangars quickly, using standard parts and unskilled labour. It was based on another standard design of joint, or node, to which steel tubes of about 3 m long could be joined to form the lattice.

Exceptionally long spans have been achieved using flat space-frames (or 'flat skeletal space grids'), as at Maidenhead: Chicago's McCormick Place Convention Center has a roof that spans 410 m x 180 m, while in Britain the roof over British Airways' 01 Hangar at Heathrow spans 135 m, with a small raised area at the end to fit the tail fins of jumbo jets. At Maidenhead Library the space-frame's span is about 30 m x 30 m, and the joints are welded.

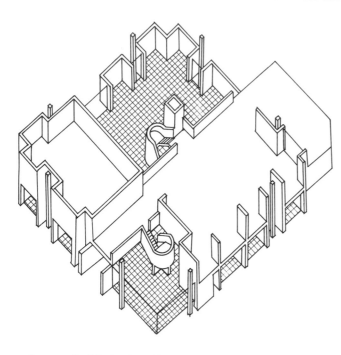

Axonometric of the interior, with the roof removed.

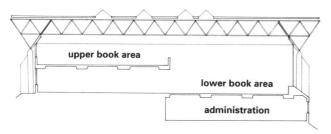

upper book area

lower book area

administration

Section, showing the space-frame covering the interior like a market-hall roof.

General view.

Pretentious prose apart, the ideas practised at Maidenhead Library gave a licence to build informally within the controlling discipline of an all-enveloping roof. This is underlined by the way in which the roof has been kept, as far as possible, separated from the brickwork below. Moreover, the notion of separation draws attention to the different functions of the roof and the walls; as if to say, 'This is the job the roof does, and this is the job the walls do – they are not doing the same job, so they should not have anything to do with each other.' (This doctrine of building elements having to be *either* one thing *or* another was being vigorously challenged at the time by the American architect and writer **Robert Venturi**.)

At Maidenhead Library the separation between the building elements is reinforced by a number of visual devices: the space-frame is supported by only eight columns, and these columns rise out of the ground outside the building's enclosing walls, which they do not touch. And, while the walls weave in and out around the building, forming themselves into little reading areas, the roof is a pure rectangle, cut off from all the busy detail of the rest of the building. Even the staircases are separate little structures on their own, standing freely within the book-rack areas.

The organization of the building is very simple indeed. The main lending facilities are on the ground floor. This is where people mill about, and the open plan helps to provide a friendly, village atmosphere, which would have been missing in a traditionally designed library full of walls and doors. Upstairs are the quieter areas, from which the main floor can be viewed in two double-height (or two-storey) 'voids'. There is also a basement accommodating the storage and staff areas, which cannot be seen from the main floor.

Robert Venturi
See Jaywick Sands, 1930 and
Aztec West, 1987 (under topic)

Chelmer Village 1974

Despite the pioneering attempts to develop an architecture that was appropriate to a suburban scale (see
Rushby Mead, 1911), the design of **suburbia** remained
a very sensitive issue. The suburban estates that had
followed the First World War had been designed
according to a housing manual that the government
had published in 1919, which put great emphasis on
keeping houses a set distance apart. This resulted in
monotony, and often led to degenerate blandness,
while attempts to integrate the motor car into the
whole pattern led to further problems. (See the discussion on Radburn planning in **Ford Estate, 1986**.)

In 1973 Essex County Council published its *Design
Guide for Residential Areas* (known as the Essex
Design Guide), which tried to set standards for the layout and design of new suburban housing estates in
the county.

The Design Guide recommended that new developments should either have a rural 'feel' about them,
in which case the landscape would dominate the
design, or an urban atmosphere, in which case the
scene would be dominated by buildings. Either way,
the aim was to promote greater variety than the inter-
war suburban designs had allowed. In the case of the
'new urban' layout, the Guide suggested that houses
could be as close to each other as 7 m, which in 1919,
when a 24 m minimum was laid down, would have
seemed like overcrowding.

The Design Guide also put great emphasis on
regional identity, and suggested that building materials should reflect the local **vernacular** tradition.

Chelmer Village, which was a commercial development begun in 1974, reflects these design values
very effectively. The houses are grouped informally
together, in what, from an aerial view, appears to be
a complete jumble. But viewed at ground level, the
village is full of intimate spaces, and each house looks
different from its neighbours.

This is a perfect solution for the developer: the
'product' (i.e. the house) appears to the purchaser to
have its own identity and a certain 'traditional' dignity
about it. For sure, terraced houses would have been
cheaper to build, and would have used the available
space much more economically, but they would have
suggested to the home buyers an unacceptable sense
of uniformity and imposed order. So, in this respect,
the design of Chelmer Village is a distortion of a more
logical design in order to sell the product, in just
the same way as the ornamentation on the front of
the houses in **51–57 Ivydale Road, 1900** was there to

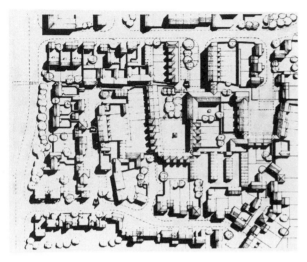

*Extract from the Essex Design Guide, showing how future
developments in the area might be laid out.*

Planning authorities
See Jaywick Sands, 1930
Suburbia
See 51–57 Ivydale Road, 1900;
Rushby Mead, 1911; North
Harrow Estate, 1925; Jaywick
Sands, 1930
Vernacular architecture
See also Hillingdon Civic Centre,
1977; Neath Hill housing in
Milton Keynes Central, 1979;
Weller Way, 1982; Burnham
Copse School, 1986; Ford
Estate, 1986; the pub and hotel
in Aztec West, 1987

sell the product, rather than to make it more comfortable to live in.

Predictably, the Essex Design Guide has been criticized by architects: to them the sense of history and tradition is false, and therefore unacceptable. But their biggest criticism is that design guides of this type are really ways of enabling buildings to get built without needing the services of architects: they are a kind of 'do-it-yourself' recipe for design, lacking the 'true creativity' of an architect-inspired scheme.

For a while the model of the Essex Design Guide was adopted by many other local authorities, regardless of whether their local building traditions were similar to those in the south east of England. But the idea has not been sustained as well as was intended: the role of local **planning authorities** in determining how new developments should be designed has long been contested, both by architects, who feel that it is their job, and by central government, which in the 1980s believed that the ultimate choice should lie with the developers: it was they, after all, who knew best what would sell and what wouldn't.

Vernacular architecture

In the early 1970s the Modernist consensus about new architecture began to be challenged. An early manifestation of this was the return to the 'vernacular' architecture of centuries ago; buildings designed in this way became known as 'neo-vernacular'.

R. W. Brunskill's authoritative *Illustrated Handbook of Vernacular Architecture* was first published in 1971. It defines a vernacular building as one that

'will have been designed by an amateur, probably the occupier of the intended building, and one without any training in design; he will have been guided by a series of conventions built up in his locality, paying little attention to what may be fashionable on an international scale. The function of his building would be the dominant factor, aesthetic considerations, though present to some small degree being quite minimal; tradition would guide constructional as well as aesthetic choice, other materials being chosen and imported quite exceptionally.'

The attraction of all this to a public, sick of the bland uniformity of the International Style, was obvious. What made it attractive to architects was that it did not require serious study to produce something in the 'vernacular' style: anyone could design an approximation of a farmyard.

Chelmer Village: each house has its own identity.

Willis, Faber & Dumas, Ipswich 1975

At Willis, Faber & Dumas all detail is stripped away from the façade, which dissolves into nothing.

This office building, in the centre of Ipswich, is in the daytime so unassertive that it merely reflects its surroundings in its darkened glass walls; but at night it is transformed into a transparent structure, in which passers-by can see the intricate workings of its interior.

The idea of creating a building apparently entirely out of glass has been one of the preoccupations of 20th-century architects. The basic technology had been mastered for the great Crystal Palace exhibition hall in 1851, but by the time of the First World War visionaries in Germany were speculating on the architectural potential of using glass alone: their designs included fiery crystals and pure, geometrical cubes of glass.

Some 50 years later Norman Foster designed the Ipswich building. It is an essay in 'minimalism': everything is stripped away from the façade until it appears to dissolve into nothing. This preoccupation with getting down to basics was always somewhere near the core of the Modern movement in architecture. It was what the German-American architect Mies van der Rohe (who had been one of the pioneers of the use of glass in building design) meant when he said that 'Less is more'.

But the problem with designing a minimalist form – as plain and as pure as possible – is that it has to be done well. At Ipswich it undoubtedly was, but as soon as the building was finished, critics began to worry that it would be copied by less thorough designers. The *Architectural Review* speculated what would happen if such buildings 'were to become, no longer the unique exception, but the norm', fearing that they would turn into a 'townscape cliché'.

Well, they did, and the mirror-glass block is now part of most British urban centres. It has come to

An example of mirror glass in London's Docklands.

signify the slickness and the facelessness of the world of commerce, as well as its impenetrability and complete lack of humour. From **Milton Keynes Central, 1979** to **Aztec West, 1987**, the image of a pure architectural form made out of glass has become a potent advertising icon, in exactly the same way as the image of rustic roofs and leaded windows has helped to sell houses for the 'volume' builders (see **Chelmer Village, 1974**).

Following the completion of the Willis, Faber & Dumas building, the next two decades were preoccupied with building huge walls of glass as elegantly as possible, without any visible means of support. In fact, the glass 'walls' of the Ipswich building have no metal frames or structure holding them up: there are 930 panels of toughened and tinted glass, each measuring 2 m x 2.5 m. They are suspended from the building's roof, and are stiffened by 'fins' of glass on the inside of the building. All of the glazed panels are butted together by a sophisticated system, which made use of the latest technology of weathertight, translucent silicone joints, and it is the technology of this jointing that has permitted so many advances in façade engineering. A comparison with the **curtain wall** of 40 years earlier at **Peter Jones, 1935** shows just how far the technology had progressed.

But there is another dimension to the Ipswich building, and that is its response to the surrounding environment. Built at a time when there was increasing call for modern buildings to be **contextual** (that is to say, to be in tune with their surroundings), it cheekily obliged by simply reflecting its surroundings. What could be more contextual than that? Its shape also conforms gently to its site, curving around the pavement in a way that a more orthodox modern building would not have done.

Contextualism
See Aztec West, 1987
Curtain wall
See Oriel Chambers, 1864; Lion Chambers, 1905; Peter Jones, 1935
Office buildings
See Bank of England, 1844; Oriel Chambers, 1864; Lion Chambers, 1905; Hillingdon Civic Centre, 1977; Crown Offices, 1980; Canary Wharf, 1990

Close-up of the glazed façade of Willis, Faber & Dumas.

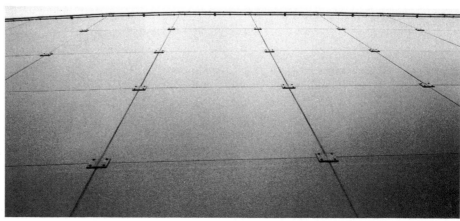

Hillingdon Civic Centre 1977

The Prince of Wales
In a speech to the Royal
Institute of British Architects
in 1984, the Prince of Wales
used the phrase 'monstrous
carbuncle' to describe a
proposal for the extension
of the National Gallery in
London. This both alerted
the world to his interest in
architecture, and infuriated the
architectural establishment
that somebody outside the
profession should dare to
talk about architecture.
In 1988 the Prince wrote and
presented a BBC Omnibus
programme entitled 'A Vision
of Britain', and followed it
with a book of the same title
(1989). After all the adven-
tures in architecture since the
Modern movement came to
Britain in the 1930s, a popular
voice was being heard –
paradoxically from the
monarchy.

As we have seen, **Manchester Town Hall, 1868** is all about Victorian municipal pomp and pride, with the mayor's office right in the centre of the building's principal façade, underneath the tower. Such an approach would be inappropriate today, however.

Hillingdon's council was only formed in 1964, out of a number of smaller authorities, and when it decided to build a new centre for its administration, it wanted a building that would convey its standing, but at the same time would be popular amongst the people who lived in what was, by and large, suburbia.

The problem that the new council and its architects, Robert Matthew, Johnson-Marshall & Partners (RMJM), faced was how to give what was really an office block an acceptable, 'human' image.

The solution they came up with is a building that has a huge, corporate interior, and a broken-up, **vernacular** exterior. It only has to be seen on a dusky evening, when the internal lighting in its strictly geometrical pattern shines through the windows, to appreciate that the building is far from the traditional farmyard it tries so hard to be. Even so, the **Prince of Wales** praised it because it 'pioneered the departure from the nuclear-fallout-shelter look for public buildings' (he had in mind buildings like the **Crown Offices, 1980**).

Taking the interior first of all: this comprises three floors of office space, with a car park in the basement and a large plant room in the roof. The office spaces are open-plan, because the council believed that enclosed small offices would lead to 'departmentalism'. Even so, every technique possible has been used to break down the vastness of these office floors. For instance, each floor has been divided into four sections, each of which has been shifted half a floor above the other in an attempt to make smaller, more identifiable work areas. By doing this, each 'quarter' of the plan has a view up or down to its adjacent sections.

At the centre of the building there are two small conservatories that rise up to the roof, in an attempt to bring the outside world (i.e. greenery) right into the office area.

Such deep-plan offices are very expensive to keep comfortable, for many work areas are far from the natural light and ventilation available at the edge of the building. This means that the building has to be **air-conditioned**, with complex arrays of pipework leading to each part of the office space, and with an extensive and expensive machinery room in the roof. Attitudes

Air conditioning

The term 'air conditioning' refers to a system for controlling the quality of air within a building, so that its rate of ventilation, its purity, its temperature and its humidity are all kept at desired levels.

Many experiments into ventilation were carried out from the middle of the 19th century onwards, but it was not until the Royal Victoria Hospital was built in Belfast in 1903 that full air conditioning was installed to maintain comfort within a building. The long, thin wards of that hospital were built side by side, so that the only windows were at the end. Conditioned air was admitted into each wall through holes placed above the beds. This air had been drawn in from the smoky Belfast atmosphere and cleaned by passing it over moist coconut-fibre ropes. It was then warmed and passed slowly along a large under-floor duct to the wards.

In 1922 the first air-conditioned theatre was built, and in the 1928 the first office block – both in the USA. Air treatment allowed for a radically different approach to building design. It could alter the shape of buildings, allowing for deep plans, where the centre of the building is a long way from the external wall. The necessity of lighting such buildings with conventional light bulbs generated much heat, which needed to be carried away by the air-conditioning system. However, by the 1950s fluorescent tubes had replaced bulbs. Not only are they more economical to use, but they emit no heat, and consequently there is need to get rid of that heat.

1 office area
2 service ducts
3 central planted areas

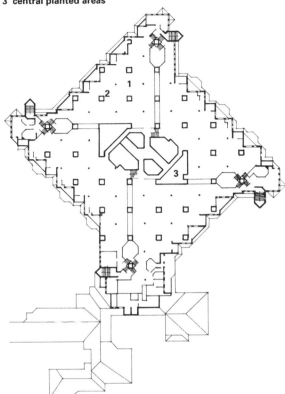

Plan of a floor at Hillingdon Civic Centre.

Detail of the cladding.

Energy

The price of oil fuel rose dramatically in the early 1970s. People also started to become more aware that a responsible attitude towards the Earth's resources was needed in any realistic policy for the future of the planet. The design of buildings is an important aspect of any energy policy. Not only do buildings consume energy for heating and lighting, but they also consume energy during construction – it takes energy to manufacture and transport all the building materials. By their very presence in the landscape, buildings can affect the climate around them, and the concentration of large office buildings in centres of population means that people need to consume more energy in reaching them (by car or other forms of transport) than in travelling to smaller, decentralized buildings situated closer to home. Laws governing the standards of building construction have increasingly tried to promote energy consciousness, and in Britain the Building Regulations demand very high levels of insulation in any new building. But to many critics this is not sufficient. A responsible environmental policy involves much more than keeping the heat in.

towards the consumption of **energy** have changed profoundly since Hillingdon Civic Centre was built.

By contrast, the building's exterior speaks of a different age and technology. Unlike the very private interior, the exterior is for public appreciation, and the architects consciously used an approach to architecture that they thought would appeal to the people who lived in this vast suburban agglomeration.

The idiom chosen was thought to be 'in keeping' with the local tradition of handmade bricks and roof tiles, and has been very carefully manipulated to form a romantic silhouette, which suggests a happy jumble of traditional buildings. At the lowest level on the façades there is a brick wall with shallow arches in it, giving the appearance is of a bridge over a venerable river, though actually the arches are there to allow ventilation to the basement car parks.

Then, above this 'bridge', the jumble of intricate bricks and roof tiles makes it almost impossible to discern the vast interiors within. Large roofs suggest great old halls, and small roofs suggest little lean-tos tacked on; but none of this is true – it is really just another office block, built all at once.

This is architecture in the service of a huge local authority, which was proud of being new and huge, but which wanted very hard not to appear to be so huge.

Vernacular architecture

See Chelmer Village, 1974; Neath Hill housing in Milton Keynes Central, 1979: Weller Way, 1982; Burnham Copse School, 1986; Ford Estate, 1986; the pub and hotel in Aztec West, 1987

Aylesbury Estate, London 1977

Defensible space

The American Oscar Newman coined this term to refer to the space immediately outside one's dwelling that one could call one's own. In traditional suburban houses, such as **51–57 Ivydale Road, 1900** or **North Harrow Estate, 1925**, the front garden is defensible space. Even where the housing is much denser, there is an element of defensible space: householders proudly maintain their front steps, and the public footpath immediately around the steps, as a means of staking out a defensible area. Newman also noted how groups of people needed defensible space, where they could collect together, and be prepared to defend its boundaries, whether real or perceived. His argument was that people need this space, and that without it housing design is inadequate.

The Aylesbury Estate in Walworth, south London, is one of the largest examples of 'system building' in Britain, having been constructed from the '12M Jespersen' system of prefabricated panels and concrete frames, which was patented by John Laing & Co.

It was designed in the late 1960s and completed in 1977, and has, ever since, been a problem for both its owner, the London Borough of Southwark, and the people who have to live in it. The estate became a byword for vandalism, and when the American academic Oscar Newman argued for **defensible space** in housing design, he cited the Aylesbury Estate as one of the very worst examples.

There can be no doubt that the area of old housing that the estate replaced was very miserable indeed. When the council set to work redeveloping the area, it was convinced that the old buildings had to come down, and that the new homes were going to be a significant improvement.

The council's optimism lay in a number of features of the design: the new scheme was to include shops, a school and a community centre – it was to be an entire neighbourhood. In addition, all the dwellings on the estate were to be heated by a 'district' heating system, in which a huge central boiler provided all the hot water; the flats were to be grouped around courtyards, to give them a sense of identifying with a particular space; each flat was to have its own garage, in a secure zone at the base of each block; pedestrians were to be kept away from traffic by providing 'pedways' at third-floor level, and the shops would be situated on these pedways; finally, next to the estate there was going to be a brand new park – the only new so-called 'Metropolitan park' to be built in London this century.

If these features gave the council confidence, each of them was soon to contribute to the scheme's failure.

As crime rose, the shops began to close. Being so far above ground level was hardly going to be good for business, anyway. The district heating scheme was very unpopular – people complained of having to pay for excess heat when they did not want it. And the long runs of heating pipes were ideal homes for vermin. The courtyards became unloved because nobody was very clear what they were for – the most popular use for them was for dumping rubbish and old cars. The garage decks were set on fire by the local kids, and then used by them as a haunt. The enterprising council soon converted them into workshops, and offices for its own architects.

The pedestrian walkways were always unpopular. The idea of walking at high level through a traffic-free environment had been suggested by the **Buchanan Report** of 1963, but it was always intended that care should be taken to make the high level a beautiful place. At the Aylesbury Estate it was not a beautiful place. In the 1980s the researcher **Alice Coleman** made a study into how certain features of housing estates promoted antisocial behaviour, and the concept of high-level pedways was near the top of her list of bad ones.

Finally, the park, which was to be connected directly to the estate's pedways by high-level bridges, never really materialized. It is there, and it is called Burgess Park, but its design hardly puts it in the same league as other Metropolitan parks like Hyde Park. The Aylesbury Estate may stand on the edge of this barren open space, but it is separated from it by a windswept road.

It is certain that no single person or even group of people should be blamed for this huge mistake. The government of the time put immense pressure on councils to use system building, arguing that speed of construction was more important than cheapness.

Eight thousand people are housed at Aylesbury, in over 2400 dwellings. With a total area of nearly 26 hectares, this gives a **density** of 326 people per hectare. It is reputed that one of the blocks on the Aylesbury Estate is the longest in Europe to be built using a construction system. There are, literally, miles of elevated walkways on the estate.

After the failure of Aylesbury, and of similar estates, the design of mass housing took a turn for the better. Architects began to search for a better solution than **high-rise** blocks: the tallest block at Aylesbury is ten storeys high, while in later estates four storeys became the norm. Great emphasis began to be given to creating defined spaces that gave a sense of community: courts that you could actually get into and streets that had an identity.

Alice Coleman

Dr Alice Coleman's book *Utopia on Trial* was published in 1985. In it she argues at great length that certain design features of mass-housing estates have been responsible for a breakdown in social behaviour, creating vandalism and damage, litter and graffiti, and leading to children being placed in care and to crime in general. Her technique is to see how the incidence of antisocial acts varies with the design of the environment. If, for example, there is more litter and graffiti in estates where there are numerically more, say, over-head walkways, then she concludes that the presence of the overhead walkways encouraged the litter and graffiti.

She has been vigorously criticized for ignoring the influence of social deprivation and poverty on behaviour, and she once told an audience that 'poverty and unemployment are not as strong an influence on behaviour as design'.

The Buchanan Report
See Lower Precinct, 1957
Density
See Back-to-Back houses, 1875
High rise
See Alpha House, 1962
Industrialized building
See Prefabricated Dwellings,

1946; Templewood School, 1949; Alpha House, 1962; Walters Way, 1987
Tenement housing
See also Boundary Street Estate, 1895; Alton West Estate, 1959; Alpha House, 1962; Aylesbury Estate, 1977; Mercers House, 1992

Herman Miller, Bath 1977

Herman Miller, the furniture manufacturers, wanted additional premises close to their existing factory on the banks of the River Avon in Bath, and they asked Terry Farrell and Nick Grimshaw to design a new building on the other side of the river, across a small footbridge.

The requirement for the new building was that it should be highly flexible, combining the functions of office space, factory and storage in a way that could be altered at any time in the future. To enable this, the building's interior is a simple grid of steel columns, separated from each other by 10 m in one direction and 20 m in the other. Steel beams up in the roof span these columns, supporting the flat roof of steel decking. All the building's services are also kept in the roof, to allow the space beneath to be completely free, and drainage runs are placed in strategic positions within the floor, so that the mobile toilet units can be moved to a variety of positions with the minimum of disruption. As far as the interior goes, the building is just a large shed, but a very sophisticated one indeed.

It is on the outside of the building that the greatest innovation can be observed: the façade is made up from glass-reinforced plastic (GRP) panels, which have been pre-coloured to match Bath stone and fitted together on a lightweight steel frame. Each panel is joined to its neighbour with a flexible neoprene gasket, so that the configuration of the wall can be changed easily, substituting doors or glazed or blank panels for each other – thus allowing the interior layout to be altered too.

The panels are arranged on the façade in two tiers, surmounted by a curved parapet. Like precast concrete (see **Preston Bus Station, 1969**), each GRP panel needs to be repeated a number of times in order to justify the effort of making the original mould. In many ways the shape of these panels reflects the nature of the material: it is a comparatively thin material, and to remain rigid the panels have to be of limited size, acquiring more strength by being curved, or having raised portions or indentations. It has to be possible to build up layers of the material within the mould, and – once set – to remove the complete panel.

The aesthetic of GRP buildings, with their rounded corners and their 'plug-in' windows and openings on the flexible façades, is more in keeping with electrical products than with traditional buildings, and this connection was very clear in the minds of the **High Tech** designers who created them.

One of the pioneers of the 'building as electrical

Detail of the cladding.

High Tech

High Tech was a short-lived style that was vigorously promoted in the early 1980s. Its popularity had been dramatically established by the Pompidou Centre in Paris (1972–7), which was designed by Renzo Piano and Richard Rogers. This building of international importance used a massive, brightly coloured structural steel frame, which was completely exposed, and it made no attempt to conceal the ducts and pipes of its servicing system. It was the consummate modern building: functional, progressive and popular.

The theme went on to be developed in a number of ways: some buildings delighted in exposing their structure and services, while others made confident use of new materials – both captured the imagination of many architects in the early 1980s.

Richard Rogers followed the Pompidou Centre with schemes like the Inmos Microchip Factory at Newport, and the massively serviced Lloyd's Building in London; Nick Grimshaw refined the use of bright, futuristic cladding panels on the exterior of out-of-town sheds; and Levitt Bernstein Associates built an exquisite 'one-off' in Manchester, placing a new theatre with an entirely exposed steel skeleton within the old Exchange building. But critics could not agree whether High Tech was really 'expressing' the 'functions' of a building, or whether it was just a style, doing what it did for the sake of appearances. In truth it was both, and High Tech, with its 'high-energy' materials and celebration of energy consumption, became increasingly associated with an irresponsible attitude towards the world's resources. It can be seen as a late fling of Modern architecture, which was already being challenged at the time by the **vernacular** revival.

Pompidou Centre, Paris: Piano & Rogers, 1977.

Vernacular architecture
See Chelmer Village, 1974

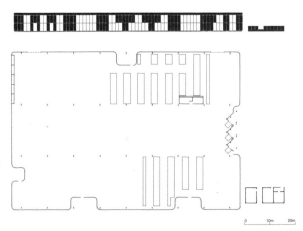

Herman Miller: elevation and plan.

product' was James Stirling & Partner's Training School for Olivetti in Haslemere (1972), which was also built with GRP panels. It exploited to the full the visual connection between the building and the product the firm manufactured. In 1982 Nicholas Grimshaw & Partners designed new studios for Wiltshire Sound Radio, making them look like a portable radio as well as being very functional as a suite of soundproof studios. In London in the late 1960s the Greater London Council had even built tower blocks that were clad in GRP panels. The system was a complete failure, however, and due to the panels' poor insulating qualities, the flats suffered from chronic condensation.

Herman Miller building, Chippenham: Nicholas Grimshaw & Partners, 1983.

The Elgin Estate, Greater London Council, 1968. Techniques developed for ambulance construction are borrowed for use in mass housing.

Olivetti Training School, Haslemere: James Stirling & Partner, 1972.

Wiltshire Sound Radio: Nicholas Grimshaw & Partners, 1982.

Milton Keynes Central 1979

The Abercrombie Plan for the future of Greater London was drawn up in 1944. It suggested the construction of ten new 'satellite' towns around London, in order to reduce the pressure on the congested inner area. After the war the New Towns Act of 1946 designated an initial 12 sites for new towns, in places like Stevenage, Crawley and Harlow. More sites followed, and in 1967 Milton Keynes was proposed, with a projected eventual population of 250 000.

Plans were drawn up, and, like all of the post-war new towns, they owed much to Ebenezer Howard's vision, which was eventually realized at Letchworth (see **Rushby Mead, 1911**). But Milton Keynes also used the American concept of 'neighbourhood units', in which the town was divided into much smaller areas, each with its 'local centre' of shops and social facilities.

An underlying discipline is vital to the design of a major undertaking like a new city, although the approach has varied through history: Howard favoured a radial geometry; in Barcelona during the 19th century, Ildefons Cerdà employed a rectilinear grid; and Le Corbusier advocated a city of tall skyscrapers standing in open spaces.

At Milton Keynes the planners devised a square grid system for laying out the city. The grid is defined by main roads, which run north/south and east/west, splitting the area up into zones of about 1 km square. Within each of the squares there is a system of smaller roads, and another system of foot- and cycle-paths, which allow people to move freely around the city with the minimum contact with motor traffic.

The discipline behind Milton Keynes allowed for piecemeal development over a number of years, and dealt with the pressing problem of road traffic right from the start.

It is possible to walk or cycle from one of the neighbourhoods to the central area without coming into contact with a road, by using the 'Redway', which is a comprehensive network of gravel paths that crisscrosses the main grid, often at a slightly sunken level. As we have seen, the idea of segregating **traffic** from people was not new (see the **Radburn System** in **Ford Estate, 1986** and the **Buchanan Report** in **Aylesbury Estate, 1977**).

The early television adverts to attract people to settle in Milton Keynes made much of its improved environment when compared, for instance, to central London.

Although each one of the grid squares has its own 'local centre' with smaller shops, the central shopping

Middleton Hall, Milton Keynes.

1 **Middleton Hall**	6 **first floor service road**
2 **Market Square**	7 **shop**
3 **Queens Court**	8 **arcade**
4 **department store**	9 **large shop**
5 **smaller retail units**	

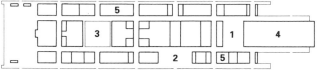

Plan of the main shopping centre at Milton Keynes, showing the retail units grouped in three rows. The service road runs on the roof.

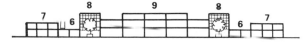

Typical section through the main shopping centre at Milton Keynes.

The Neath Hill Local Centre.

area contains the largest concentration of shops in the city. Like the whole city, the design of the central shops follows a very strict discipline. Seen from above, the complex is divided into three rows of retail units. The two outer rows contain smaller units, while the central row houses the largest stores. The rows are separated by two tall pedestrian arcades, which in two places open out into 'squares', one of which is covered, while the other is open.

In traditional developments shops have a public frontage with entrances and display windows, and a private rear for servicing and loading. At Milton Keynes the loading area is on the first floor, so that once again heavy traffic is kept out of sight and clear from pedestrians. This first-floor service road runs around the entire complex, so that it has access to every shop.

The architecture of the complex is very much of its time. Its steel frame is not disguised (except where it has to be encased for fireproofing purposes), and the outer skin of the building is a simple grid of glazed panels. It provides a very airy atmosphere within the arcades, and a clean, uncluttered look to the outside. It has, however, been criticized because it looks like a building of no particular function, rather than a shopping centre.

Like many new British developments, especially London's Docklands, Milton Keynes shows a startling contrast between the urban architecture of its commercial areas, and the architecture of its housing. For example, the Neath Hill neighbourhood of Milton Keynes, with its **vernacular** styling, was built at the same time as the 'Shopping City', but could not be more different from it.

local centre

The Neath Hill neighbourhood: the thick broken line is the Redway; the Local Centre is marked; the other major buildings are schools.

Pedestrians and traffic	Meadowhall, 1990
See also Lower Precinct, 1957	**Vernacular architecture**
Stores	See Chelmer Village, 1974;
See also Selfridges, 1907;	Hillingdon Civic Centre, 1977;
Peter Jones, 1935;	the pub and hotel in Aztec West, 1987

Crown Offices, Cardiff 1980

This building, occupying such a prime position in a capital city, was built in a short-lived architectural style known as brutalism, which earned it nothing other than public hostility. When it was completed, a critic wrote that the building conveyed estrangement and distance, lending 'an impression of bureaucracy under siege'.

Its chief interest to us lies in the external form, and the effect it has on us all. This style of architectural treatment became popular for large buildings, from office blocks to civic playhouses, from the 1960s onwards. In this respect, the Cardiff building is a late and uninspired example of the type. Not only are there the obligatory Modernist icons of a recessed ground floor and absolutely no surface ornamentation, but there also seems to be a delight in producing harsh and almost brutal forms.

The **Prince of Wales**, in describing Birmingham's central library, built in a similar idiom in 1973, wrote: 'It seems to me like a place where books are incinerated, not kept! . . . It is an ill-mannered essay in concrete "brutalism" intended to shock.'

The term 'brutalism' had been coined in the early 1950s to describe a particularly British expression of Modern architecture – that is, a rebellion against the politely genteel forms of the Festival of Britain. Much brutalist thinking came from the later work of **Le Corbusier**, who had built the very influential monastery of La Tourette near Lyons in 1955, and whose forms can be seen crudely reinterpreted at Cardiff.

In Britain the brutalist era was coincidental with the early films of Ken Loach, and shared some of their directness in its wish to get to the truth of things by exploiting raw building materials frankly and without affectation. The movement could be seen to have its apotheosis in the new buildings of London's South Bank arts complex of 1965–8. It is strange that the popular **Royal Festival Hall, 1951** should have as its new neighbours examples of architecture that specifically challenged it. Externally the Hayward Gallery and the Queen Elizabeth Hall have always been deeply unpopular. 'Who would guess,' wrote Lionel Esher, 'that those gloomy bunkers were built to celebrate the pleasures of the senses?'

In the Cardiff building's defence, it is not designed for public access, unlike the South Bank arts complex. Mounted high on its walls are video monitors that track an intruder's every movement. Within its ground-floor colonnade the impression is one of power: in this respect the building has classical qualities, and is not

View along the colonnade which runs around the Crown Offices building. Compare with the Altesmuseum opposite.

dissimilar to the grand colonnades of Karl Friedrich Schinkel's great classical buildings of the 1820s in Berlin.

It certainly looks like a fortress, the upper floors pierced by slit windows, and a kind of a moat around the base. The comparison with **Hillingdon Civic Centre, 1977** is interesting. Both buildings are large administrative offices and there are many similarities between them. Despite this, the Hillingdon building appears to be open and welcoming, while the Cardiff one seems the exact opposite – alienating and enclosed. This comparison proves the persuasive power of architecture, which can achieve such a strong contrast and effect through the external articulation of a building.

Internally the two buildings have more in common. They both rely on open-plan office layouts, for instance. In the Cardiff building five floors accommodate 2500 people, of whom 80 per cent work in the open-plan office, while the remaining 'higher-grade' personnel have enclosed, 'cellular' offices. Inside the entrance there is a large 'atrium', clad in travertine with generous planting, and throughout the building there is plush carpeting and ash panelling. There is also a 'landscaped water garden' opening off the coffee lounge, full catering facilities, a library and a cinema. Again, as at Hillingdon, the Cardiff building is fully **air conditioned**. It was a very expensive building to construct, and is very expensive to run.

La Tourette, near Lyons: Le Corbusier, 1960.

The Hayward Gallery, in the South Bank arts complex, Waterloo, London.

The colonnade in the Altesmuseum, Berlin: Karl Friedrich Schinkel, 1822.

Air conditioning
See Hillingdon Civic Centre, 1977
Le Corbusier
See Wicklands Avenue, 1934; Templewood School, 1949; Alton West Estate, 1959
Office buildings
See also Bank of England, 1844; Oriel Chambers, 1864; Lion Chambers, 1905; Willis, Faber & Dumas, 1975; Canary Wharf, 1990
The Prince of Wales
See Hillingdon Civic Centre, 1977

Weller Way, Liverpool 1982

The appalling conditions of derelict 19th century street housing; the impersonal local authorities whose institutional **tenement blocks** were almost impossible to move out of; and, in London at least, the takeover of inner-city land by big business so that new cheap housing could no longer be built – these factors caused many **community** groups in the 1970s and 80s to fight for the right to get homes built, against all the odds. The Weller Streets Co-op in Toxteth, Liverpool, is just one example.

In his introduction to *The Weller Way* (1986), Alan McDonald describes the development as

'a small modern estate quite unlike anything around it. Groups of six or seven houses in ruby-red brick are set in ten L-shaped courtyards, where bushes and shrubs are pushing up among the few parked cars. It looks like rented housing, regular and utilitarian, but it has a private, secluded feeling to it too. You don't quite feel you can wander in through the pathways, but you don't quite feel excluded either.'

In 1977 the residents of the run-down Weller Street area had formed a co-operative, and five years later, after fighting a tenacious struggle against bureaucracy, their new estate – Weller Way – had been built. With the help of a local architect, the members of the co-operative had participated in the design of the new homes, and in so doing had demonstrated what a wide gulf there is between what people actually want from the environments they live in, and what up till then they had always been given by design professionals. At one point they had stated to Bill Halsall, their architect: 'We design the buildings; you hold the pen.'

The members of the co-op did not want the architecture of their new homes to remind them of the terraced streets they had put up with for so long. They associated terraces with slums. The old Weller Street area had jokingly been called 'a great tourist spot – you could see the cathedral from the outside toilet'. And, as a reaction against those conditions, the residents just 'wanted to leave them streets . . . and surround ourselves with a wall and gun turrets'. They were also quite clear that they did not want their new homes to be anything like the old flats that Liverpool Corporation ('the Corpy') had built. The uniformity and scale of the design of these great estates were associated with municipal paternalism, with its ability to assemble large areas of land for housing development. Reaction against the forms of these earlier schemes frequently

---

Tenement blocks
See also 145 Buccleuch Street, 1892; Boundary Street Estate, 1895; Alton West Estate, 1959; Aylesbury Estate, 1977; Mercers House, 1992
The Prince of Wales
See Hillingdon Civic Centre, 1977

Community architecture

The 'community architecture' movement grew in the late 1970s out of disparate battles for control of the development of land. In London the battle for Covent Garden had halted the wholesale demolition of old buildings, but did not halt the gentrification of the area; the 'Battle for Tolmers Square' did not prevent an old housing area being turned into a slick mirror-glass office block; while at Coin Street in Waterloo the community campaigned for, and won, the right to build homes in the very heart of London's commercial centre. In each of these struggles architects played key roles on behalf of the local communities, often at great risk to their own livelihoods. They were even attacked by their own profession, and in 1978 the then President of the Royal Institute of British Architects (RIBA) had to agree not to take action against architects who had been offering their services for free to local communities, instead of charging the mandatory scale fee.

By 1979 the first community technical aid centre was established in Manchester, and by 1983 a national grouping of such centres (the Association of Community Technical Aid Centres) was formed. But the establishment was quick to get in on the act, and RIBA set up its own community architecture office; at one point a community architect/entrepreneur even became the President of the Institute.

The **Prince of Wales** was also getting involved, and in 1986 he launched the 'Building Communities' conference at the Astoria Theatre in London. The conference was sponsored by a large commercial developer, and really marked the point at which the community movement gained respectability as part of the establishment. Large architectural practices began to specialize in this kind of work, and built national reputations out of it. But despite this, the entrenched positions of power within the politics of building procurement remained unchallenged. As the great architect Sir Edwin Lutyens once put it: 'Architecture, more than any other art, represents the intellectual progress of those that are in authority.'

figured in the wishes of the co-op.

The decision to divide the scheme into courts was partly due to this, and when two of the courts chose to use the same colour of brick, the co-op's management committee initially refused to accept it, saying that too much use of the same brick would make the scheme look like a 'Corpy' estate.

It was always intended that the two-storey courts should be intimate and semi-private in character, so as to discourage intruders (see 'Defensible Space' in the **Aylesbury Estate, 1977**). The feeling of intimacy was a fundamental aim of the new design, but it was a different sort of intimacy to that which is so often attempted in commercial housing schemes, where the underlying purpose is to make each household look in on itself, and shun the idea of a shared community.

At Weller Way the courtyards with their generous landscaping are genuinely shared. Even so, it has been difficult in practice to decide whose responsibility it is to maintain the planted areas, especially those that are very close to the houses. In 1993 the decision was taken to cut back on the communal planted areas, and to give the dwellings small front gardens.

1 **front door**
2 **planting and car parking**

Plan of Pine Court, Weller Way,
showing the extent of the
communal planting.

Burnham Copse School, Tadley 1986

Throughout the 1980s new schools and public build-ings designed by the Hampshire county architects' department achieved a great deal of recognition, and received a number of awards. Burnham Copse, com-pleted in 1986, is just one of a long line of new schools in the county, and is no more noteworthy than many of the others, but it does demonstrate both an approach to architecture and to school planning that is typical of its time.

The school stands in the middle of Tadley, a town of housing estates between Basingstoke and Reading. It is not an inner-city area, and this school's architec-ture, like many of the others in the county, is about open space and traditional suburban values.

Even so, the two conical roofs are not unassuming, and were deliberately chosen to give some character to the low-key surroundings. We are free to make any associations we like when we look at the building: a wigwam, or a big top or fairground, and not necessar-ily a school. In this way, Burnham Copse is completely unlike an old Victorian Board school with its large win-dows and high walls, and conventional architectural values (see **Primrose Hill School, 1885**).

In fact, the two major roofs are clear indications that the building is a school, because they stand over the two principal spaces inside – the hall and the shared teaching area. Furthermore, the most public space, which is the shared area, has the highest roof,

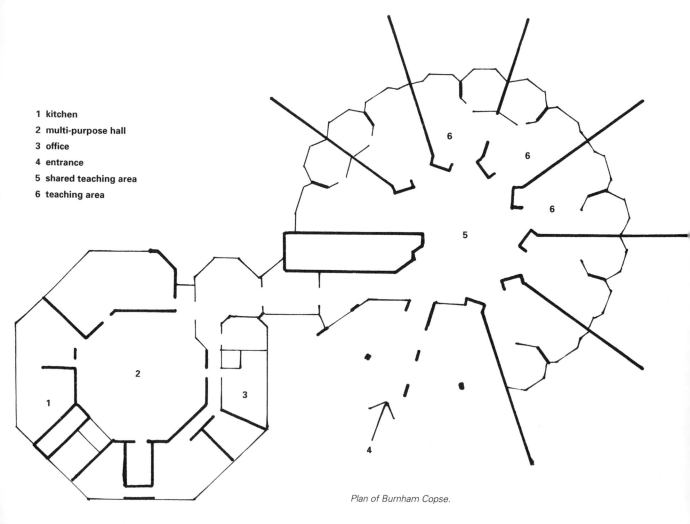

1 kitchen
2 multi-purpose hall
3 office
4 entrance
5 shared teaching area
6 teaching area

Plan of Burnham Copse.

while the most private spaces, which are the individual classrooms, have the lowest.

Despite its very individual appearance, the planning of Burnham Copse's teaching spaces embodies thinking in school design that goes right back to the pioneering Hertfordshire schools of the post-war period (see **Templewood School, 1949**). This is that there should be a main shared area, which would be the space through which people walk as they move around the building; and leading from the shared area should be all the classrooms, which in turn have their own direct connection with the outside play areas.

But Burnham Copse is not quite 'open plan', for the classrooms are separated from each other by walls, while their connection to the central shared area is left open. The result feels very informal, and uninhibiting to small children. However, openness in school design does have its problems, and this often requires the teachers to set strict rules about how the buildings are to be used.

Being inside the central shared area is like being in a tent: there is a view right up to the apex, and slatted timber panels have been fitted to the inside to give a smooth appearance to the conical ceiling. This contrasts with the character of the other major roof over the hall. Here, the timber structure has been left exposed, and the blank side walls divide this central space (which can be used as a gym) from the more private places like offices and the music room.

The importance of the two major spaces, and the way in which the smaller spaces have been fitted around them, indicates that the building was, by and large, designed from the inside to the out. In other words, the external composition was not as important as the way that the internal spaces fitted together – exactly as we saw at Templewood School. Once again, this contrasts with more traditional school design, in which external composition was often of prime consideration.

The Hampshire schools and others like them occupy a very special place in British modern architecture: they are modern, because they are planned to serve a very well understood function, and because they do not follow the rules of classical composition. But they are also very sensitive to their surroundings and respectful of **vernacular** architectural values. In some respects, then, they represent a taming of the harshness of early Modern architecture, and they belong to an altogether wider tradition.

Architect's model.

Detail of the roofs.

Shared teaching area.

Interior of the multi-purpose hall.

Vernacular architecture
See Chelmer Village, 1974; Hillingdon Civic Centre, 1977; Neath Hill housing in Milton Keynes Central, 1979; Weller Way, 1982; Ford Estate, 1986; the pub and hotel in Aztec West, 1987

Ford Estate, Wirral 1986

The Radburn system
In the 1920s part of the town
of Radburn in New Jersey,
USA, had been designed by
Clarence Stein and Henry
Wright using the principle of
differentiating the fronts and
the backs of dwellings: the
cars would be kept in open
courts at the back, which had
access to the road system,
while the front doors would be
connected to the town's
network of footpaths. The two
systems were kept entirely
separate. After the Second
World War the Dudley Report
was published, which had
strongly recommended that
new housing estates be
designed on the Radburn
principle, and it was used
in much post-war housing
development in Britain –
particularly in council-
developed 'peripheral' estates,
away from town centres.

Thirty years is a long time in the life of a house, and a very long time in the lives of the people who live in it. The Ford Estate had, by the mid-1980s, become the most unpopular estate in the Wirral.

Consisting of over 2000 homes, it had been built from the mid-1950s onwards using a non-traditional technique of construction that was not destined to last long. The 'cross-wall' technique used sturdy walls to separate each of the dwellings along the terrace from each other, but flimsy panelled walls for the front and back of each house. By the 1980s the cross-walls were still sound, but the front and back walls, which were only made of timber framing, were in very poor condition, badly insulated and needed replacing.

Another technique used when constructing the estate was the **Radburn system** of planning – a device for keeping **traffic and pedestrians** separate. But like so many theories, the Radburn system did not work well in practice: there was no problem with the appearance of the front of the house, but at the rear there was a large area of tarmac. What is more, the system led to tremendous confusion: if visitors called on foot, they would arrive at the front door of the house; but if they came by car, they would have to park at the back, then walk through the back garden to the back door. This flew in the face of the ritual of entrance that had been established so effectively in British house design (see **51–57 Ivydale Road, 1900**).

Not surprisingly, in view of the faulty design of the Ford Estate, the residents suffered as the result of increasing crime and vandalism, along with more graffiti and dumping; they did not pay their rents, and tried their hardest to get out of the area.

Traffic and pedestrians
See also Lower Precinct, 1957;
Aylesbury Estate, 1977; Milton
Keynes Central, 1979

Both cars and pedestrians now have access to the fronts of the dwellings at Ford Estate.

1 **pedestrians**
2 **cars**
3 **cars and pedestrians**

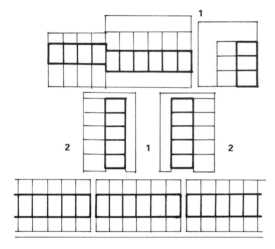

Ford Estate as built in 1956, showing the segregation between traffic and pedestrians according to the Radburn system.

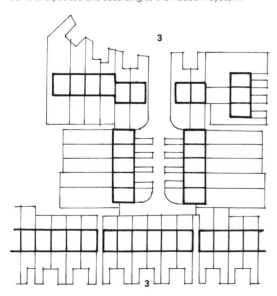

Ford Estate as redeveloped in 1986, with some of the houses 'turned'.

The council finally decided to take action in the mid-1980s, and started a comprehensive redesign of the estate. Nearly all the buildings were kept, but their appearance changed so radically that it is now impossible to tell what they once looked like.

The Radburn layout was eliminated. Instead of separating the cars from pedestrians, they were both allowed access to the fronts of the houses. This meant that the rears of the houses could now be private gardens, with no risk of strangers entering. The unpopular car-parking courts were grassed over to make space for these gardens. As for the cars, they were given spaces right at the front of each dwelling, so that they could be overlooked from the dwelling itself, instead of being out of sight in some distant court.

In order to achieve these changes, some of the dwellings needed to be 'turned', so that their old backs became their new fronts.

The most profound change was in the buildings' appearance: the flimsy panelled construction was removed and replaced with well-insulated brick walls. The long, horizontal, 'modern'-style windows were replaced with a more traditonal hardwood variety, with smaller glazed areas and much better insulation. Horizontal brick bands were introduced above and below these windows, and porches were added to the new fronts of the houses.

The remodelling of the Ford Estate was hailed as a great success, and was cited by the government as an example of good practice.

Walters Way, London 1987

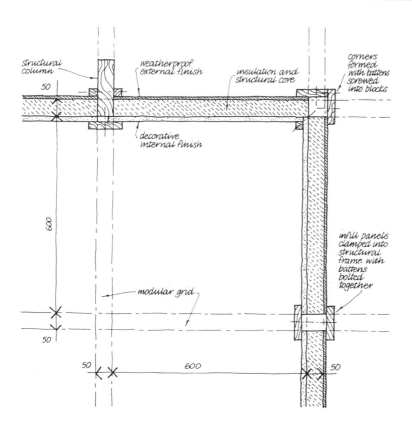

structural column
50
weatherproof external finish
insulation and structural core
corners formed with battens screwed into blocks
decorative internal finish
600
modular grid
infill panels clamped into structural frame with battens bolted together
50
50   600   50

Building systems

See also Prefabricated Dwellings, 1946; Templewood School, 1949; Alpha House, 1962; Aylesbury Estate, 1977

Walters Way: the 'tartan grid' allows a 50 mm structural zone, and a 600 mm zone for panels.

The houses in Walters Way, in south London, were all built by their occupants using the 'Segal' method. This comprehensive approach to building was developed by the architect Walter Segal when he wanted to construct a temporary home for himself and his family in 1962. It allows unskilled people to make their own homes using simple materials and techniques. The method is also suitable for different types of building, including schools and offices.

The method is very flexible, and buildings that use it can be altered at will, because the main structure of the building is a timber frame. All the external and internal walls, the floors and the roof are fixed to this frame, and are not structural.

The key to the design is the 'tartan grid'. This is a geometrical pattern that defines where the frame and the panels can go. It is called a tartan grid because it is made of pairs of parallel lines that cross each other at 90 degrees. The parallel lines are 50 mm apart – which corresponds to the thickness of the main frames –

while each pair of lines is 600 mm from the next pair. This is the most commonly available width for building panels and boards. Columns and beams and panels can be designed to fit at any appropriate point on this grid.

All 'wet' activities like concrete-making and plastering are kept to a minimum. The foundations are simple holes in the ground filled with concrete, and capped with a paving slab. The timber frames are fixed together on site using hand-held power tools, and are laid flat upon the ground. They are then hauled up one by one and gradually fixed together with cross-members.

The roof is put in place as soon as possible, so that all subsequent building can be done in a degree of comfort. Flat roofs are often used in the Segal method, and they are of simple construction. The waterproofing is done by bonding together layers of roofing felt, and this is one of the few operations that probably needs skilled help. While most housing designers

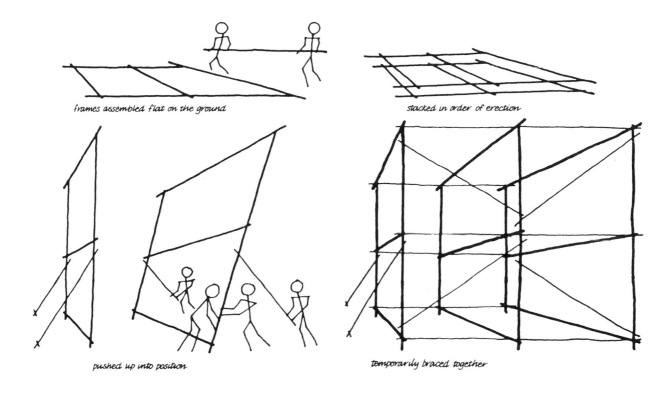

frames assembled flat on the ground

stacked in order of erection

pushed up into position

temporarily braced together

Walters Way: the main frames are assembled using hand-held tools and then erected in position.

were turning away from flat roofs, since they needed much maintenance and tended to leak, Segal vigorously advocated them. He even suggested that, in the self-build houses, they were laid completely flat and without the usual slight slope to help the rain run off: if they stayed wet, this did not present too much of a problem, for it helped to keep the roof at a constant temperature.

Following the Segal method, walls are not structural and they can be put in place after the roof. They are built using a number of different panels sandwiched together. Segal called these panels the 'raincoat', the 'sweater' and the 'vest'. The outer panel, or raincoat, keeps the weather out; the middle panel, or sweater, is insulation, keeping the warmth in; and the 'vest' panel is the internal finish, which might be plasterboard or pinboard. Each of these panels is supplied from builders' merchants in 600 mm widths, so that it can easily be co-ordinated within the structural frame. When the panels are in position, they are

gripped to the rest of the structure by two vertical strips of timber, one outside and one in, which are bolted together.

The internal walls are fitted in roughly the same way. Again, this can all be done using simple tools.

Buildings constructed using the Segal method have a varied, but very distinctive, architectural character. They look light, though not insubstantial, and it has been suggested that they also look optimistic, as if they represent a revolutionary new way of building. The attractions are obvious: almost anyone can build a Segal home, and some progressive councils have gone out of their way to ensure that no would-be self-builders are held back for financial reasons.

But critics of the system say that, for all its qualities, it is not a way to build whole cities. The architecture of the Segal method is, if anything, about the power of the individual. It is not about social living on a civic scale.

Aztec West, Bristol 1987

Business parks have evolved rapidly in Britain. They were modelled on USA schemes like Silicon Valley in California, where firms specializing in computing and information technology removed themselves from inner-city locations to cleaner, quieter and cheaper surroundings away from the city.

In Britain in the early 1980s 'high-tech' computer-based industries wanted their entire operations under one roof, and they naturally gravitated towards the new, more spacious out-of-town locations. The concept of business parks became even more popular when the government changed its planning laws in 1987, allowing for a blurring of the distinction between office space and industrial space, so that the new parks could become flexible mixes of the two functions. As a consequence, the exclusively electronics make-up of the early parks gave way to a variety of businesses, attracted by the marketing of the parks that lay emphasis on their pleasant layout and environment.

Many of the new developments, like Stockley Park (near Heathrow) – which is built on an old rubbish tip – make use of so-called 'brown' land, or land which was previously industrial but which has now fallen derelict. All of them are located as close as possible to a convenient motorway intersection. Arlington Estates' Aztec West business park was built near where the M4 and M5 motorways intersect, about 12 km to the north of Bristol city centre. It is laid out with courtyards and lakes, together with wine bars, leisure clubs and cafés, and it tries to re-create the atmosphere of the city centre out in the countryside.

Often called 'the Village' by the people who work there, Aztec West is described by its developers as the place 'where business is a pleasure', and their marketing material makes great play of its attractiveness.

In reality it is what has been termed an 'architectural zoo', with business premises in many different architectural styles nestling behind neat landscaping around the orderly circular distributor road. The whole layout is geared towards the motorist, and efficient signposting makes it difficult to get lost. Access to all of the buildings is by a series of culs-de-sac, which lead off the ring road, and landscaped parking spaces are placed adjacent to each entrance.

The park offers a textbook of British architecture of the 1980s – most contemporary styles are represented, and so too are buildings that show concern for **energy** saving and sustainability. Most of the buildings are **High Tech** sheds, whose designs are brash and colourful, with much use of reflective glass and

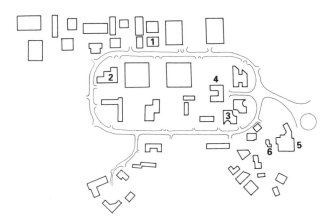

Plan of Aztec West.

1 (see p. 158) units
2 (see p. 161, bottom illustration) units
3 (see p. 160, top illustration) units
4 Aztec Centre
5 hotel (see p. 160, middle illustration)
6 pub (see p. 160, bottom illustration)

The work of Campbell, Zogolovitch, Wilkinson & Gough has done much to elevate the drabness of London's Docklands. These units at Aztec West are in a similar vein.

The hotel at Aztec West.

The Black Sheep pub, Aztec West.

exposed angular metal structures. Their air-handling
equipment is also frequently exposed, emphasizing
not only their modernity, but also the semi-industrial
nature of what goes on inside.

Many other buildings within the park are brick-
built, and once again the emphasis is on up-to-the-
minute style, with frequent **Postmodern** references to
historical architecture. But this is all in great contrast
to the architecture of the hotel and the Black Sheep
pub out on the east side of the park. Instead of being
dynamically stylish, these have been built in a way
that suggests tradition and domesticity. The pub in
particular could not jar more with the High Tech sheds
behind it, even though it is as new as they are.

Surrounded by 'instant' landscape, with hanging
baskets and a tiled roof complete with decorative
finials, the interior of the Black Sheep has a stone-
flagged floor and ceilings lined with old wooden
beams, and there is even a gas flame flickering in the
Victorian cooking range. The illusion is well done, and
only the over-bright brasswork and the piped music
that disguises the hum of the fans give the game
away.

Aztec West seeks to re-create all that is attractive
about the traditional town centre. Its architecture is
dynamic, and that is to its credit; but no town or city
can develop overnight, especially when it is geared so
exclusively to the motor car. How can it sustain its
illusion when there is nobody living there – no old
people, or schoolchildren skipping by? The only out-
of-hours life is that of the security guard doing his
rounds among the manicured planting.

*National Gallery Extension, London:
Venturi and Scott Brown, 1991.*

*The Isle of Dogs Pumping Station: John
Outram & Partners, 1988.*

*John Outram & Partners designed these units at Aztec West in a
very similar idiom to their Pumping Station on the Isle of Dogs (see
above), a building that was celebrated by the Prince of Wales with
the comment: 'At long last!'.*

Postmodernism

The term 'Postmodernism' has been widely misinterpreted within architecture: many architects think that all it implies is the superficial use of historical motifs. But Postmodernism is a much wider cultural phenomenon – present in the cinema, in literature and even in politics. Within architecture it applies to an overthrow of the Modern movement, a rejection of Modernism's austere doctrine of no-frills functionalism. The Modern movement saw its buildings as objects in space, while Postmodern buildings help to create a continuity of space – they appear less alien in their surroundings and attempt to be 'contextual' (see reference in **Willis, Faber & Dumas, 1975**).

Postmodernism is pluralistic: it permits different people to 'read' buildings in different ways. This is distinct from Modernism, where only one interpretation of a building is possible, on the basis that the building is no more than a logical expression of its functions. Postmodernists believe that architecture is a series of signs, which people interpret according to their own personal set of experiences. They therefore have no objection at all to the use of historical forms, like those of **classical** or **vernacular** architecture, for these forms are widely understood and therefore allow buildings to 'communicate'.

Postmodernists also value the use of humour – buildings are allowed to play tricks on the viewer. There can be false doorways, or oversized elements; the jokes can be understood by absolute beginners, or they can be reserved for those 'in the know'. One of the most famous Postmodern buildings is **Robert Venturi**'s extension to the National Gallery in London. It is so loaded with historical references, and so humorous, that it has been condemned by the more straight-laced of the architectural establishment. The Isle of Dogs Pumping Station, designed by John Outram, is another exuberant example. The **Prince of Wales**, in his *Vision of Britain* book (1989), said of it: 'At long last! John Outram has been brave enough, on the Isle of Dogs, to design a pumping station which soars beyond functionalism and enters the world of witty and amusing symbolism.' Outram's units at Aztec West are very similar.

Robert Venturi

The Philadelphia architect and writer has probably been the most influential architectural thinker of the 20th century after Le Corbusier. His first book, *Complexity and Contradiction in Architecture* (1966), presents a vigorous denial of the 'monovalent' values of Modern architecture. One of the most famous phrases of the book was a retort to the Modern architect Mies van der Rohe, who had said that 'Less is more' (in other words, keep designs minimal). Venturi countered this with 'Less is a bore' – in other words, make designs complex and rich. In a similar vein the book also argues for elements of architecture to be *both* one thing *and* another, in contrast to Modern architecture's either/or approach (see **Maidenhead Library, 1973**).

In the house that he designed for his mother in 1962, he built a staircase that was also a bookshelf. The joke was that the staircase led nowhere. This philosophy presented a fundamental challenge to Modern architecture, for to Modernists things had to be clearly stated, and honest. Jokes were definitely out. In 1972 Venturi's second major work, *Learning from Las Vegas*, appeared. Written jointly with Denise Scott Brown and Steven Izenour, it analyses the Las Vegas strip, looking at the way the buildings and the roadside signs next to them actually communicate.

Classical architecture
See Bank of England, 1844
Energy
See Hillingdon Civic Centre, 1977
High Tech
See Herman Miller, 1977
The Prince of Wales
See Hillingdon Civic Centre, 1977
Vernacular architecture
See Chelmer Village, 1974

Meadowhall, Sheffield 1990

1 large store
2 food court
3 mall

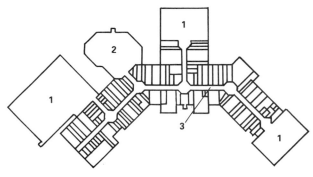

*Plan of the upper shopping level at Meadowhall. The malls run
through the centre of the building, with smaller units on either side.
At changes of direction there are large, domed spaces containing the
escalators and lifts. At the end of the malls are the 'anchor' units –
the large department stores.*

Exterior of Meadowhall: blank walls in a sea of car parking.

If the architecture of **Milton Keynes Central, 1979** is
anonymous, and lacking in glitz, Sheffield's Meadowhall is a move in the opposite direction. The comparison between the two is very instructive.

Shopping complexes are a recent phenomenon.
They can be defined as managed complexes of trading
units, served by controlled pedestrian circulation
routes and fed by a transport system (usually the
motor car). Of course there are links back to earlier
models of grouped shopping: the bazaar, the arcade
and the street market. Profound changes came with
industrialization, as mass demand was fuelled by
developments in packaging, advertising, food distribution and food preservation.

In North America, where there was plenty of available land, shopping centres in out-of-town locations
flourished, but in Europe the first examples appeared
in bombed or derelict parts of the inner city. Pioneering British schemes were built in the early 1960s at the
Elephant and Castle in Southwark, and in Birmingham's Bullring.

Meadowhall, on the site of an old steelworks
5 km out from the centre of Sheffield, followed the
precedents set by West Edmonton Hall in Alberta,
Canada (1981–5), and the Metrocentre in Gateshead
(1987) in providing a wide range of attractions, including a leisure complex, under one roof.

The planning of all of these retail centres follows a
basic logic: retail units of varying size, from large
stores to smaller units, are all grouped around central
shopping 'malls'. These malls are made to be just like
conventional streets (without the traffic), and in some
cases they are actually designed to look like conventional streets. The difference is that the fronts of the
shops face the malls, and their backs face the outside
world. The urban problem posed by most shopping
complexes (Milton Keynes is an exception) is that their
façades are actually their rears. Meadowhall is very
conspicuous, and it was an important asset to its
developer that it could be seen from an elevated por-
tion of the nearby M1 motorway. But close to, its architecture consists of blank walls and loading bays.

It is like a building turned inside out. Its principal
public face is on its interior, while externally it gives little to its surroundings – it has over 2 km of external
façade, much of which comprises service yards and
the rears of shops. The complex sits in two levels of
car parking, from which it is possible to enter the malls
at both first and second shopping level. At each of the
changes of direction of the malls there is a glazed

dome, under which are the golden lifts and escalators (We saw in the **Lower Precinct, 1957** how going upstairs has to be made a pleasant experience before people will choose to.) It is a make-believe environment, recalling various themes, from classical and exotic architecture to a Spanish village, complete with Spanish street names.

The attraction of complexes such as Meadowhall lies in 'one-stop' shopping. To make them viable, they must have a number of 'magnet' or 'anchor' units – the big-name stores – to bring people in. There is also an increasing use of leisure complexes on the same site to provide a further attraction.

At the West Edmonton Hall the leisure complex is right in the middle of the shopping area, but at Meadowhall it is in a separate structure a few hundred metres away. In Gateshead's Metrocentre the leisure facilities are at the end of one of the malls – in the same prominent position as a large store – including a fully functional roller-coaster.

The architectural treatment of these huge shopping complexes is also very important in attracting customers. The architecture of Meadowhall is like background music: it is not the architecture of the mall but the store frontages facing the malls, with their full-height windows, that are designed to be the main focus of attention. The centre itself only provides the coherent framework.

The stark style of the Milton Keynes complex is generally no longer favoured. Even worse were the pioneering centres such as that at the Elephant and Castle, which is a faceless box marooned in traffic.

The aesthetic of the brick and pitched roof is now in favour, along with traditional features that suggest that the great malls are just extensions of the traditional city centre. This they certainly are not. The city centre has always been the place where many functions come together, and a huge concentration of varied activities can take place, not just those of a commercial nature. As we have seen, the point can be made just as strongly at **Aztec West, 1987**, and the two developments are both symptomatic of the erosion of city centres in the late 20th century. In malls such as Meadowhall there are no civic, cultural or residential ingredients – such places are all about spending and consuming. Their architecture offers only the thinnest of suggestions that they are part of the traditional city.

Gateshead Metrocentre's 'Metroland' leisure facilities.

Stores

See also Selfridges, 1907; Peter Jones, 1935; Lower Precinct, 1957; Milton Keynes Central, 1979

Canary Wharf, London 1990

The Canary Wharf development is a collection of buildings standing on the Isle of Dogs, just to the east of the City of London. One of the buildings – the Canary Wharf Tower – is the tallest in Europe. The development is significant for two reasons: it shows an approach to design known as 'master planning', in which one designer takes responsibility for the overall layout of the project, while the design of individual buildings within that layout is undertaken by different firms. In this way there is variety within the whole development, and the illusion is created that it has been constructed over a period of time.

Canary Wharf is also significant because of the various forms of architectural language that it uses, and the enormous effort that has been taken to clothe the buildings with architectural styling. It is an awesome place to visit.

In 1981 the government set up the London Docklands **Development Corporation** (LDDC) and charged it with the responsibility of redeveloping the dock area, which had lain derelict since the 1960s. In the Isle of Dogs (not really an island but a peninsula) the LDDC established an 'enterprise zone' – which is planning jargon for saying that any viable business can set up shop in the area without having to ask for planning permission in the usual way, and without having to pay the council tax.

To begin with, only small commercial buildings were erected in the enterprise zone, but as the economic boom of the 1980s got under way, larger developers became attracted to the area. The key site was always Canary Wharf, which was the location on the Isle of Dogs that was closest to the established commercial centre of the City.

The developer, Olympia & York, settled on a master plan for the 28.5 hectare site that envisaged 26 different buildings, grouped into four 'neighbourhoods', each of which has its own public open space. The key building in all this is the Tower, standing in the middle of a huge axis that runs the width of the Isle of Dogs. In the words of the developers: 'Here is a sublime statement of confidence in the new district, proclaiming the conviction that Canary Wharf and London's future are indissolubly wedded, full of promise and potential.'

The architecture of the 240 m high Tower is simple – the window design repeated endlessly throughout its height. It was designed by the American Cesar Pelli, and its architecture is unmistakably American in inspiration, coming in a direct line from the Empire State

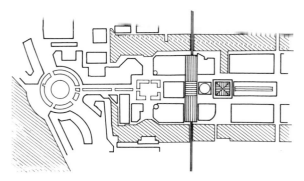

Plan of the development at Canary Wharf.

Development corporations
See BDC Marketing Centre, 1992
Office buildings
See also Bank of England, 1844; Oriel Chambers, 1864; Lion Chambers, 1905; Willis, Faber & Dumas, 1975; Hillingdon Civic Centre, 1977; Crown Offices, 1980

No. 10 Cabot Square.

Building and the Rockefeller Center in New York.

The foundations are formed by 222 concrete piles, each sunk to an average depth of 18 m below the ground level, and above this the structure of the building is a steel frame, which grew out of the ground at an astonishing rate – at its fastest, a storey a week. In plan it is a perfect square, with sides of 58 m. At the core of the plan are banks of 32 lifts, with a special 'jumbo' lift in the middle, as well as other services. The pyramid at the top contains lift machine rooms, and mechanical and electrical plant rooms.

Unlike the Tower itself, many of the smaller buildings around it have an applied architecture that is classically inspired, recalling the very earliest commercial blocks of Chicago. On first appearance they look to be stone-built, with traditional elements like rusticated bases, pedimented windows, corner cupolas and roof gables. But, like the Chicago blocks of nearly a century earlier, the Canary Wharf buildings are actually constructed with a steel frame. The 'stonework' that covers their façades is only a few centimetres thick. In fact, it is in most places reconstituted stone, or even concrete.

Most eyecatching, and severely classical, of the smaller buildings is No. 10 Cabot Square – a massive building in its own right. The story goes that the British prime minister of the time was so fooled by the illusion it created that she congratulated the developers for 'not demolishing one of the original buildings'. At the centre of No. 10 Cabot Square is a nine-storey atrium, which, it is claimed, has similar acoustics to St Paul's Cathedral.

This slick, American-style 'grey-suit' business architecture has its place alongside that of the shopping mall, the school and the housing estate. It is, just like any other, an architecture that is designed to appeal, for a particular purpose. But the purpose of this architecture is very clear indeed: it is to attract commercial tenants to the scheme, and to create the illusion that the area has the solidity of a well-established financial centre. To quote the developers once again: 'We believe that Canary Wharf is the place where every far-sighted company will want to make its home.'

Early commercial developments on the Isle of Dogs: Heron Quays, designed by Nicholas Lacey, Jobst and Partners in the mid-1980s.

BDC Marketing Centre, Bristol 1992

Development corporations were established by central government from 1981 onwards in order to promote investment in run-down areas. They became planning authorities in their own right, with the power to give planning permission to any development proposal they wished, and they took this responsibility from locally elected councils. It was not surprising that they were heavily criticized: their boards were not elected and they often took no account of local needs and opinions.

Sometimes the architecture they sponsored was also questionable: in London the LDDC (see **Canary Wharf, 1990**) allowed some very poor urban planning and buildings.

That criticism at least cannot be levelled at the Bristol Development Corporation (BDC), as far as its Marketing Centre is concerned. Commissioned from the Alec French Partnership, it was designed to symbolize the start of commercial regeneration in an area of the city that is still largely blighted. The elegant structure stands like a beacon on the bank of the River Avon.

The symbolic nature of visitor centres and marketing centres is extremely important. In Limerick (which, like Bristol, is situated on a major river), on the west coast of Ireland, the building there borrows its imagery from boats, complete with rigging and sails. At Cardiff the development corporation created a huge telescope of a building: through its one end-window visitors could see all the way across the bay.

At Bristol the location was very different. The building is set low in a river valley, where the only possibility of a view is from a height. This justifies its main architectural gesture – a giant blue mast, from which all the accommodation is literally hung.

In the early 20th century the design of ships was put forward as supremely functional for building design. Their horizontal, white superstructures, their handrails and round portholes were copied on buildings by the 'pioneers' of the Modern movement, even though what might have been appropriate for a ship, with its need to stay afloat on a turbulent sea, might not be applicable to buildings. Since then, the metaphor of ship design has continued to be attractive to building designers, especially in recent times when **High Tech** was fashionable, with its masts, its cables and its exposed ventilation equipment.

At the Bristol building all the main spaces are organized radially from the mast, and the lowest floor is suspended about a metre above a shallow pebble-lined pool. This lowest level is the main reception area, where visitors can see audio-visual presentations. Or, if they prefer, they can climb up the outside of the building, on to a series of round platforms attached to the mast. Because of the way they are suspended, these upper platforms sway slightly, reinforcing even further the suggestion of boats and the maritime history of Bristol.

The building was designed to be moved to a new site every three or so years, which meant that the form of construction used had to be simple to dismantle and re-erect. Each of the main radial structural members folds up to the central mast for transportation by lorry; it is a mechanism that is easy to understand when one examines one of the principal joints.

Although a sailmaker was used to construct the canvas awnings, and there is much use of natural wood in the building – all the external decks are made from west African opepe – the external walls and the roof employ very sophisticated modern 'sandwich' construction techniques, in which an outer weatherproof 'skin' is separated from the internal skin by a layer of insulation. The building may have been designed to be moved, but it is also able to provide an energy-saving internal environment, which is now a requirement of law.

(Far left) BDC Marketing Centre: the timber decks on the upper platforms are suspended above the riverside.

The central mast at BDC Marketing Centre, with the special folding arrangement that allows the building to be transported by lorry to a new site.

High Tech
See Herman Miller, 1977

Mercers House, London 1992

Bond

For most of the 20th century,
builders have used cavity
construction when building
with bricks. This is where the
wall is split into an inner and
an outer 'leaf', with an air gap
in between to improve
thermal insulation and prevent
water penetration. As the
outer leaf is usually only 100
mm wide, only 'stretchers' (or
the long face of the brick) are
visible. This 'stretcher bond'
leads to a rather uniform
appearance. Hence, to achieve
a more pleasing visual effect,
cut bricks were laid in the
walls at Mercers House, to
give the impression of
headers.

Detail of a doorway.

By the middle of the 1980s serious attempts were
being made by architects to return to the architectural
values that had prevailed before the Modern movement. This suited both conservative ideologies, which
believed that there was a 'correct' architecture (rather
as one might believe in a 'correct' way of speaking
English), and liberaideologies, which saw modern
architects as remote and élitist, creating buildings to
appeal to fellow-architects, as opposed to the population at large.

The **Prince of Wales**'s influential book *A Vision of
Britain* (1989) had done much to legitimize the return
to more traditional architectural values, and as a result
it infuriated the architectural establishment, which
was still largely promoting the doctrine of Modernism.

Mercers House, in the East End of London, is an
admirable illustration of how a new architecture can
arise from a careful and passionate study of the past.
It makes no attempt to be progressive, concentrating
more on the need to communicate with and be understood by the people who pass it and who live in it.

It is actually a complex of two buildings: a
separate doctors' surgery occupies a side street and
the housing block is on the main Essex Road. Its planning is quite utilitarian: separate entrances lead from
the street to staircases, with access to two flats on
each landing. This follows the 'walk-up' type of design
(see **145 Buccleuch Street, 1892**). The flats, which
house elderly residents, are simply and comfortably
planned, with a communal social room and laundry,
and one permanent warden for the whole of the block.

But it is on the outside that Mercers House has its
greatest impact. The architect, John Melvin, has used
a series of 'quotations' from architecture of the previous century or earlier, and reinterpreted them in a
design that is altogether of its own day. Chasing the
sources of all the quotations is an interesting exercise:
Melvin has admitted to a particular affection for the
works of Frank Lloyd Wright, William Butterfield and
H.S. Goodhart Rendel, and a good many more
besides.

But the key point is that the influence of the Modern
movement has all but disappeared. There are arches
over the entrance doors, and horizontal string courses
picked out in concrete (in the 18th century they used
stucco to pretend to be stone; concrete makes a much
better imitation). At the top of the building there is a
cornice, which is a much more satisfactory capping for
a brick wall, both in functional and aesthetic terms,
than the simplistically plain details preferred by the

Modern movement. The building materials in Mercers House have been used in a way that demonstrates an intimate knowledge of their properties: parapets and sills properly spill the rain away from the walls below, and therefore stop them being stained – brick and carefully precast concrete age well, but the flimsy devices used by modern architects to keep buildings artificially plain do not.

In the external walls of Mercers House the brickwork even uses a **bond**, with both headers and stretchers, not just because this looks traditional, but also because it looks good. It is a building in which immense care has been taken in its crafting, both inside and out.

After the frantic search for a 'new' architecture that has persisted throughout the 20th century, Mercers House has been a great relief to describe. Its architecture is only a short step away from that of the **Boundary Street Estate, 1895**, whose architects also prided themselves on their careful, sensible and delightful use of materials. This work has been appreciated by a much wider audience than just architects, whose negative judgements have so often been difficult to comprehend.

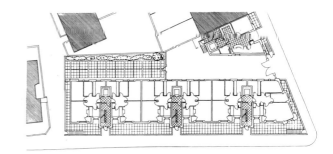

Plan.

The Prince of Wales
See Hillingdon Civic Centre, 1977

Tenement housing
See also Boundary Street Estate, 1895; Alton West Estate, 1959; Alpha House, 1962; Aylesbury Estate, 1977

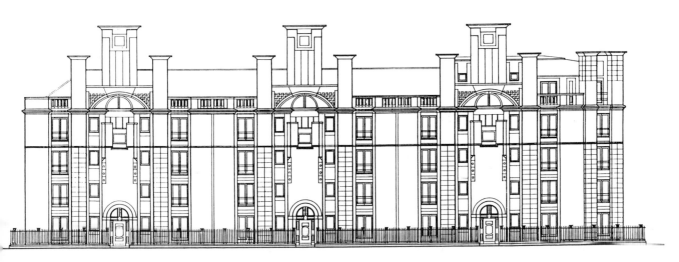

Elevation to Essex Road.

Glossary

aedicule

The use of ornamentation to make a doorway, window or niche look like a little building in its own right, with a pair of columns on either side, and a pediment above. See p. 5, middle illustration.

arch

An arch carries the load of the structure above an opening, taking the weight down either side of the opening. Arches are usually formed from pieces of stone or from bricks, which are laid on *formwork*. Apart from the familiar semicircular arch, favoured by the *classical* Romans, there are also pointed arches (as in *Gothic* cathedrals); segmental arches (segments of a circle); and even flat arches, in which the top and the bottom edges are flat, but the stones or bricks are wedged tightly together to give structural strength.

art deco

As a decorative movement of the 1920s, art deco is associated more with interior and product design than with architecture. However, its curvaceous forms were occasionally found on the exterior of buildings like the Odeon cinemas (see p. 103, illustration).

art nouveau

A decorative movement of the 1890s, characterized by sinuous curves and wave- or plant-like forms. Mainly centred in Paris

and Brussels, its principal British exponent was Charles Rennie *Mackintosh* in Glasgow.

arts and crafts

The movement towards simplicity and truth to materials pioneered by William *Morris* from the late 1870s. See *Boundary Street Estate, 1895*.

ashlar

Building stone that is cut with straight edges and built in regular, horizontal courses (as opposed to *rubble*).

atrium

Traditionally applied to the courtyard of a classical Roman house, the term 'atrium' has in recent times come to be used to describe a tall void, often fully enclosed and landscaped, in the centre of a large commercial building. See *Crown Offices, 1980* and *Canary Wharf, 1990*.

attic

In *classical* architecture, a top storey of a building, above the *entablature*.

axis

An imaginary line passing through a building, around which the building may be planned.

axonometric

A precise, three-dimensional drawing in which the *plan* of the building is not distorted, and all the verticals are drawn to scale. It is easier to draw and easier to measure from than an *isometric*.

(the illustration at the top of p.122 is also an axonometric.)

Baroque

A 17th-century trend within architecture and other arts that use *classical* forms in a very exuberant way. In Britain the work of Sir Christopher Wren was the prime example.

Barry, (Sir) Charles

(1795–1860). Following a 'grand tour' of Europe, he designed *Gothic* churches. The Travellers and Reform clubs (1831 and 1837) helped to establish the *palazzo* mode for urban buildings. In 1839 his most famous design – for the Houses of Parliament – started to be built. Much of its *Gothic* detail was designed by *Pugin*.

basilica

In Roman times the basilica was a building designed as a meeting place, and the word came to apply to the typical Christian church form, with its high central nave and two lower side aisles.

battle of the styles

See *Manchester Town Hall, 1868*.

Bauhaus

A progressive school of *arts and crafts* had been established in Weimar in Germany in 1906, and in 1919 Walter *Gropius* became its director, renaming it the Bauhaus. It became the century's most important school of design, and played a key role in establishing the 'machine

aesthetic' of *Modern* architecture. Gropius designed new buildings for the school at Dessau in 1925 (see p. 91, bottom illustration).

bay

A structural division, in the horizontal plane. In a cathedral a bay goes from one major column to the next.

bay window

A curved or angular projection containing a window, usually in a house. See *51–57 Ivydale Road, 1900*.

bond

The way in which bricks or stones are laid in a wall, so that they can bind together to give the wall overall strength. The different types of bond can be distinguished by the pattern of *stretchers* and *headers* that they make. See also *Mercers House, 1992*.

brickwork

See *The Granary, 1869*.

brutalism

Originally used to describe *Le Corbusier*'s later works of the 1950s – e.g. Unité d'Habitation (p. 113, bottom illustration) and La Tourette (p. 145, top illustration) – it became a British movement characterized by the South Bank arts complex (p. 145, bottom illustration), with harsh forms built in rough-finished concrete. See also *Crown Offices, 1980*.

building regulations
In Britain these are regulations that set standards of construction for any new development. They deal with the building's structure, fire safety, sound transmission, ventilation, hygiene, drainage, heating, stairways and the conservation of energy.

Butterfield, William
(1814–1900). Most of his buildings were churches. He used the *Gothic* idiom very inventively, employing brilliantly coloured brick. His masterpieces were *All Saints, Margaret St, 1855* and Keble College, Oxford, 1870.

cantilever
A building element that projects horizontally without supports at its outer edge, the tendency to topple being resisted by restraints behind the 'fulcrum', or pivoting point. See *Ibrox Stadium, 1928.*

capital
The element at the top of a column that transfers the load of the *entablature* down on to the column. The capital is the most ornate, and instantly recogniz-able, element within *classical* architecture. See p. 9, bottom illustration.

casement window
A simple window in which the hinges of the opening part are along its side.

cladding
When the external skin of a building is not structural, it is known as cladding.

classical/classicism
In architecture, the buildings of

Greece (*c.*600–300 BC) and Rome (*c.*100 BC–AD 300), and the architectural philosophies that they inspired. See *Bank of England, 1844.* See also *neoclassicism.*

classical orders
See *Bank of England, 1844.*

Coade stone
A popular type of artificial stone, similar to *terracotta*, that was invented by Mrs Eleanor Coade in the late 18th century.

Commissioners' church
A church that was built as a result of Acts of Parliament at the beginning of the 19th century, to bring religion to the urban poor. See *All Saints, Margaret St, 1855.*

compression member
An element of a structural system (like a post or a strut) that works by resisting its two ends being pressed together (as opposed to a *tension member*).

concrete
A building material created by mixing water with cement and an 'aggregate' like sand or pebbles. See *in situ concrete*, *precast concrete* and *reinforced concrete.*

corbel
An element of a building that projects outwards to support another element.

Corinthian order
One of the *classical orders.* See p. 9, bottom illustration.

cross-wall construction
A technique used in repetitive

housing design, in which all the loads of the building are carried by the separating walls only.

curtain wall
Originally, the outer defensive wall of a castle, but in the 20th century it refers to a non-structural external wall of glazed or translucent panels. See *Peter Jones, 1935.*

deck access
(or gallery-, balcony-, or open access). A system of access in a *tenement* block. See *145 Buccleuch Street, 1892.*

Doric order
One of the *classical orders.* See p. 9, middle illustration.

elevation
A drawing of one of a building's vertical faces, in which all the measurements are accurate. Drawings like the Banqueting House, p. 4, are elevations.

entablature
The massive, horizontal element supported by columns in *classical* architecture. See p. 9, bottom illustration.

faience
Glazed decorative pottery or earthenware.

formwork
(or shuttering). Usually timber, or less often metal or plastic, on to which stones or bricks are laid as arches or vaults, or into which concrete is poured. Once the structure has been created, the formwork is usually taken away.

frontage
In housing design, the width of the dwelling as it faces the street. Hence 'narrow frontage' and 'wide frontage' houses.

functionalism
The belief, popular from *c.*1920–70, that a building should only reflect the function it is supposed to perform.

garden city
A development like Letchworth, based on Ebenezer Howard's principles. See *Rushby Mead, 1911.*

garden suburb
Smaller than a garden city, and developed on the outskirts of a large town, Bedford Park (started in 1875) was the 'pioneer' garden suburb (see p. 71, illustration).

Gaudí, Antonio
(1852–1926). The most famous Catalan architect, renowned for his wildly exuberant and colourful buildings in Barcelona. Other architects were working in a similar way at the same time, but Gaudí had the advantage of enjoying the patronage of Count Guell, who commissioned his best buildings.

Georgian architecture
Nothing to do with who happened to be on the throne at the time, this phase of architecture, *c.*1750–1850, is characterized by the *Palladian* terraced house (see *Hamilton Square, 1830*).

girder
A major beam, usually in a floor, which supports other elements of structure.

glass-reinforced plastic (GRP)
See *Herman Miller, 1977.*

golden ratio/section
The ratio of 1:1.618. See *Templewood School, 1949.*

Gothic
The architectural style of the Middle Ages, *c.*1100–1500. The *Gothic* revival started in the late 18th century. See *All Saints, Margaret St, 1855.*

grid lines
Imaginary lines used by the building designer to discipline the building's organization. See *Templewood School, 1949.*

Gropius, Walter
(1883–1969). German-American architect who pioneered the 'machine aesthetic'. Works include the *Bauhaus* design school in Dessau (see p. 91, bottom illustration), of which he was director. Like many other German architects, he fled from the Nazis during the Second World War and came to Britain, before finally settling in the USA to practise and teach at Harvard University.

Guimard, Hector
(1867–1942). French *art nouveau* architect, best known now for the highly ornamental entrances to the Paris Métro stations, *c.*1900.

header
A brick whose short side is visible when laid in a wall. See *bond.*

High Tech
See *Herman Miller, 1977.*

High Victorian Gothic
An inventive but very principled interpretation of *Gothic* prevalent in the 1860s. See *All Saints, Margaret St, 1855.*

Horta, (Baron) Victor
(1861–1947). Belgian architect who, in the 1890s, produced many *art nouveau* buildings.

in situ concrete
(or 'in its place' concrete). Concrete that is moulded in its final position – as opposed to *precast concrete.* See *Lion Chambers, 1905.*

International Style
The style associated with *Modern* architecture, *c.*1910–70.

Ionic order
One of the *classical orders.* See p. 9, bottom illustration.

iron
See *Albert Dock, 1845* and *Newcastle Central Station, 1850.*

isometric
A precise, three-dimensional drawing in which the lines of the plan are drawn at an equal angle to the horizontal (usually 30 degrees). Although the plan is distorted, it gives a more realistic representation than an *axonometric.*

jack-arch construction
See *Albert Dock, 1845.*

Jones, Inigo
(1573–1652). Having visited Italy, he brought the architecture of that country, and *Palladio* in particular, to Britain. His most famous buildings are the Queen's House in Greenwich (1618) and the Banqueting House at Whitehall (1622 – see p. 4). See *Hamilton Square, 1830.*

Le Corbusier
(*né* Charles Édouard Jeanneret, 1887–1966). A Swiss-born French writer, poet, painter and architect, who helped to pioneer the sleek white *Modern* aesthetic. In the 1950s he adopted a broader palette of materials, which helped to inspire *brutalism.* Probably the most influential architect of the 20th century. See p. 113, bottom illustration and p. 145, top illustration.

Lethaby, William Richard
(1857–1931). An English architect known more for his inspired teaching than his buildings. Greatly influenced by *Shaw, Webb* and ultimately *Morris,* he promoted the teaching of crafts in the Central School of Arts and Crafts, of which he was the first principal.

Lutyens, (Sir) Edwin
(1869–1944). Highly original, more than influential, English architect. In the 1890s his succession of houses and courts, many in south-east England, combined *vernacular* forms and sensitive landscaping with inventive architectural composition. He designed New Delhi, the Indian capital, in 1913.

Mackintosh, Charles Rennie
(1868–1928). Scottish artist and architect who started working in the *art nouveau* idiom in the 1890s. He designed the Glasgow School of Art in 1896.

mansard roof
A roof, usually at the top of tall urban buildings, which has two pitches: the lower part is steeply pitched, and the upper part has a shallower pitch.

Mendelsohn, Erich
(1887–1953). German architect whose earliest designs were fantastic curvilinear sketches that were never built (see p. 79, illustration). The Einstein Tower observatory in Germany is the closest he got to realizing those visions. He created influential designs for department stores (see p. 90, middle illustration) and cinemas in Germany, before fleeing to Britain in 1933, where he had a short career before moving on to Israel, and finally to the USA.

Mies van der Rohe, Ludwig
(1886–1969). Before leaving Nazi Germany, Mies van der Rohe had been an early visionary of glass architecture (see *Willis, Faber & Dumas, 1975*), and had pioneered 'no-frills' *Modern* architecture, as in the Barcelona Pavilion of 1929. His career flourished in the USA after the Second World War, perfectly detailed Modern university buildings, houses and office blocks. His most famous words were 'Less is more' (see *Robert Venturi* in *Aztec West, 1987*).

Modernism/Modern movement
Broadly, the ideas behind the most vigorous development in architecture in the 20th century. See *Wicklands Avenue, 1934.*

module
A repeated unit of measurement, used in the design of a building. See *Templewood School, 1949.*

Modulor

A system of measurement and proportion devised by *Le Corbusier* in the 1940s and 50s, and based on the proportions of the male figure and the *golden ratio*.

Morris, William

(1834–96). Influential English socialist, propagandist, author and designer who believed that all art should be 'by the people and for the people'. His own designs, and his house (designed for him by Philip Webb) were romantically rooted in the Middle Ages, and for all Morris's influence and intentions, his position was ultimately bourgeois, as opposed to revolutionary.

Nash, John

(1752–1835). An English architect who was equally at home with picturesque and exotic architecture, like Brighton Pavilion, as with the white *stucco classicism* of the Regent's Park terraces, all of which he designed in the 1810s and 20s.

neoclassicism

The use of the *classical* language of architecture has increased and decreased in popularity for thousands of years. The *Renaissance* (see *Hamilton Square, 1830*) marked a new era of classicism, but the particularly austere use of Greek forms in the late 18th/early 19th centuries is known as the neoclassical period. See p. 9, bottom left illustration.

new towns

See *Milton Keynes Central, 1979*.

open plan

See *Wicklands Avenue, 1934*.

orders, classical

See *classical orders*.

oriel

A type of *bay window*, protruding from an upper floor.

palazzo

A great merchant palace situated in the centre of an Italian town. See *Hamilton Square, 1830*.

Palladio, Andrea/Palladianism

Andrea Palladio (1508–80), and the movement that he inspired. See *Hamilton Square, 1830*.

Parker & Unwin

Barry Parker (1867–1941) and (Sir) Raymond Unwin (1863–1940) helped to design the first *garden city* at Letchworth (see *Rushby Mead, 1911*). Unwin became a very influential town planner.

Parker Morris Report

In 1961 the Parker Morris Report, commissioned by the government, laid down new and generous standards specifying the minimum space requirements for all new housing design.

pediment

The triangular, roof-like structure at the top of a *classical* portico.

Pevsner, (Sir) Nikolaus

(1902–83) German architectural historian who came to Britain, where he dominated the field for three decades. A vigorous campaigner for Modern architecture, he ruthlessly interpreted history to prove the justification for and inevitability of *Modernism*. His greatest

works are *Pioneers of Modern Design* (1936), *An Outline of European Architecture* (1943) and the encyclopaedic 'Buildings of England' series, in which the architecture of every English county is described.

philanthropy

In the context of buildings, the charitable provision of housing. See *Akroydon, 1861*.

piano nobile

The principal living floor of a *palazzo*; usually the first floor, with the largest windows.

pilaster

A flat *classical* column placed against the surface of a wall.

plan

A measured drawing giving an 'aerial' view of a building, usually with the roof or upper floors removed.

polychromy

The use of many colours in the construction of a building. Polychromy was an important aspect of the *High Victorian Gothic* phase. See *All Saints, Margaret St, 1855*.

portico

(or temple front). The entrance of a *classical* temple, with a base, colonnade and pediment. The most frequently employed building motif. See *Bank of England, 1844*.

precast concrete

See *Preston Bus Station, 1969*.

prefabrication

See *Prefabricated Dwellings, 1946*.

Pugin, Augustus Welby Northmore

(1812–52). English architect who converted to Catholicism in 1834, and argued thereafter for a 'true', 'Christian' (and therefore, in his mind, Catholic) architecture, which to him was encapsulated by the architecture of the *Gothic* period – a style that he understood profoundly. He worked with *Barry* on the design for the Houses of Parliament.

Radburn system

A way of separating vehicles and pedestrians in housing estates. See *Ford Estate, 1986*.

Queen Anne revival

See *Primrose Hill School, 1885*.

reinforced concrete

To make *concrete* strong in tension as well as in compression, steel reinforcing bars are laid into position before the concrete is poured into the mould. Now, as reinforced concrete, it can be used as a very efficient building material. See *Lion Chambers, 1905*.

Renaissance

The 'rebirth' of *classical* values and forms that occurred in the early 15th century, replacing those of the medieval period. See *Hamilton Square, 1830*.

render

The plaster coating on a wall.

rubble

Irregular-shaped building stones (as opposed to regular *ashlar*).

Ruskin, John
(1819–1900). English theoretician who, through his books, argued for high principles in architectural design, especially through careful study of medieval architecture, and in particular Venetian *Gothic* (*The Stones of Venice*, 1853). He abhorred the 'vulgar' architecture that sprang up in the London suburbs as a result of his works, calling the buildings 'accursed Frankenstein monsters', and argued for the intensely middle-class 'good taste' of fine craftsmanship.

rustication
Masonry given a rough appearance to look like heavy stones, with deeply grooved joints between them; mostly used on the lowest parts of *classical* buildings.

sash window
A window that opens by sliding one of its two glazed panels, or sashes, up or down. The sashes are counterbalanced by weights.

Scott, (Sir) Giles Gilbert
(1880–1960) Apart from Battersea Power Station, his best known work is the competition winning scheme for Liverpool's Anglican Cathedral. His grandfather, (Sir) George Gilbert Scott (1811–1878), was England's most prolific builder and restorer of *Gothic* churches, and also designed the Foreign Office in London in the *Renaissance* idiom (see *Battle of the styles*).

section
An accurate drawing of a building's interior, after it has

been cut vertically. The bottom illustration on p. 106, is a section.

Segal method
The method devised by Walter Segal in Britain, which allows people to build cheaply, and with the minimum of skills. See *Walters Way, 1987*.

Shaw, Richard Norman
(1831–1912). The most influential architect in late-19th-century Britain and the leading practitioner of the *Queen Anne revival*. In addition to Bedford Park suburb (p. 71, illustration) and the White Star Offices (p. 45, top illustration), he built a number of important office buildings and houses in the 1870s and 80s.

shuttering
See *formwork*.

space-frame
A flat, latticed roof structure that is capable of spanning in all directions (a beam only spans in one direction). See *Maidenhead Library, 1973*.

spandrel
Correctly speaking, the space in a wall immediately beside the curve of an arch. More recently (as used in *Selfridges, 1907*), a spandrel panel has come to mean a panel placed between repeated windows on the façade of a tall building.

stretcher
A brick whose long side is visible when laid in a wall. See *bond*.

string course
Raised horizontal band or course of bricks on a building.

stucco
A form of *cement* that is used for covering walls. It was frequently used on the external walls of *Georgian* buildings, and moulded into ornamental forms, especially as an imitation of stonework.

temple front
In *classical* architecture, another term for a *portico*.

tenement
A dwelling within a larger block. See *145 Buccleuch Street, 1892*.

tension member
An element of a structural system that works by resisting the forces which try to pull its two ends apart (as opposed to a *compression member*).

terracotta
See *Manchester Town Hall, 1868*.

Thomson, Alexander
(1817–75). Known as 'Greek' Thomson, he was a Glasgow architect working in a *neo-classical* Greek idiom, which he developed very freely. See p. 10, illustration.

Tuscan order
One of the *classical orders*.

Venturi, Robert
See *Aztec West, 1987*.

vernacular revival
See *Chelmer Village, 1974*.

Vitruvius
Active *c*.50 BC, this Roman architect achieved influence from the *Renaissance* onwards simply because his rather dull book on

architecture had survived. It was then translated many times by architects, each of whom used it to promote a particular position within the *classical* revival.

walk-up access
A form of access in *tenement* blocks. See *145 Buccleuch Street, 1892*.

Webb, Philip
(1831–1915). An English architect whose first and most important work was the Red House, which he designed for his friend William *Morris* in Bexleyheath in 1859. His subsequent work was exclusively domestic, and often very close to contemporary schemes by *Shaw*.

Wright, Frank Lloyd
(1869–1959). The most inventive and original American architect of his time. His very varied output includes some magnificent private houses from the early 1900s in the Chicago area, followed by larger schemes like the Johnson Wax Factory (1936) and the extraordinary spiral Guggenheim Museum in New York (started in 1942).

Index